REALITY-BASED PARENTING

How Parents of African Descent Can Cultivate Loving Relationships With Their Children

Sponsored by:
Center for Psychotherapy
813 Maple Street
Brooklyn NY 11203
PH 347 244 7258
info@center-for-psychotherapy.com
www.center-for-psychotherapy.com

John P. McQueen, ED.S, LCSW, CFLE

Copyright © 2015 by John P. McQueen, ED.S, LCSW, CFLE.

ISBN: Softcover   978-1-5144-0168-2
       eBook   978-1-5144-0167-5

All rights reserved. No part of this book may be reproduced or transmitted in any form or by any means, electronic or mechanical, including photocopying, recording, or by any information storage and retrieval system, without permission in writing from the copyright owner.

Cover Design: Lozanodesign.com (212) 255 6829

Adinkra symbols developed by the Ashanti people of Ghana, West Africa can be traced back to the 17th century. The symbols in the book are from www.adinkra.org

Any people depicted in stock imagery provided by Thinkstock are models, and such images are being used for illustrative purposes only.
Certain stock imagery © Thinkstock.

Print information available on the last page.

Rev. date: 11/16/2015

To order additional copies of this book, contact:
Xlibris
1-888-795-4274
www.Xlibris.com
Orders@Xlibris.com
714629

Table of Contents

Dedication vii
Acknowledgments ix
Preface xi
Introduction xiii
Contributing Authors xv

1. Love Without Fear: How Parents of African Descent Can Build Effective Relationships with Children 1
2. Roots and Wings: Foundations For Parenting African-American Children (Part I) 11
3. Roots and Wings: Foundations for Parenting Children of African Descent (Part II) 19
4. Personal Philosophies for Parents of African Descent 31
5. Playing to your Child's Strengths 37
6. Parenting styles: A guide for Nurturing Children of African Heritage 45
7. The ABC's (Awareness Behaviors Change) of Child Development 57
8. Disciplining for Dignity: Rewards and Consequences 65
9. Effective Communication: How to Talk so Children Will Listen and Listen, so Children Will Talk 73
10. Learning Outside the Classroom: Transcending Artificial Boundaries 85
11. How Parents of African Heritage Can Cope with Stress (Part I) 94
12. How African-American Parents Can Manage Stress (Part II) 105
13. Co-Parenting for the Best Child Outcomes (Part I) 116

14. The Fatherhood Factor: Impact
    of a Father's Absence (Part II) 123
15. Money Management Basics for Parents & Children of
    African Descent (Part I) 135
16. Money Management Basics for Parents of African
    Descent (Part II) 145

Appendices 153
Index 195

Dedication

------- O -------

Ambition is the desire to go forward and improve [our] condition [by improving the lives of our children]. It is the burning flame that lights up the life of our [children] and makes [them] see [themselves] in another state. To be ambitious is to be great in mind and soul [and to transmit same to our children]. [Ambition] is to want that which is worthwhile [for us and our children], and to strive for and maintain it. [It is] to go on without looking back, reaching to that which gives [fulfillment and] satisfaction … (Marcus Garvey).

In the spirit and power of Marcus Garvey we dedicate this book to Sonia Hart, Ronald Richardson, Sandra Watson, Charlene Williams, Floreen Cox, Amoy Williams, Dele Adebara, Benedict Brizan, Yvette Moore, Lumine Damour, Maria Theodule, Antoinette Broadnax, Muba Yarofulani, Kimberly Anderson, Akilah Holder, Sandra Gunpot, Bertram Hart and Glenda Perreira, initial participants in our inaugural Reality-Based Parenting class, September 2001. Their support, enthusiasm, inspiration, parental practices, and feedback were the impetus for writing this book.

Acknowledgments

------- O -------

The African adage, "It takes a whole village to raise a child," characterizes the collaborative manner in which this book was compiled. Indeed, it took a village to have brought this offering to fruition. In the self-same spirit of our ancestors, I hereby acknowledge the people who helped with this project in ways that far exceeded the call of duty.

I must first thank, of course, the 19 contributing authors (see contributing authors in the table of contents) for their inspired writing especially with regards to the vital cultural/spiritual component and who have spent a great deal of time and effort crafting their work for a specific audience – African-American parents. One of the chief complaints made about parenting books intended for parents of African descent is that they are often too general. Our contributing authors attempted to fill this void. Reality-Based Parenting is indeed a refreshing departure from most of the existing literature.

Next on the list is Center for Psychotherapy's administrator, Ms. Lorraine Oudkerk, for offering critical institutional support without ever once uttering a word of complaint. She exemplifies outstanding leadership. I thank her for her steadfast encouragement, support, and flexibility for being able to juggle between her personal commitments, family life, and work obligations. Likewise, I am grateful to Professor Elaine Reid (Medgar Evers College Field Education Coordinator) for sending me an exceptional social work intern, Pauline Melchoir, who immediately conceptualized Center for Psychotherapy's project goals and provided invaluable research, coordination, support, cooperation and the indefatigable energy required for completing this oft-exasperating project. Her professional assistance in helping to successfully execute this project is greatly appreciated.

I acknowledge professor Norissa Williams, PhD, Naila Smith, MA, and Nadege Waithe, MSW for their exceptional editorial assistance. Their efforts, dedication, and sacrifice were evident in their meticulous work. I am grateful that they were willing to contribute to this special project. Special thanks to Kenson McQueen and Brandon Jimenez for researching parental quotations and helping to compile Reality-Based Parenting glossary, respectively. Also, a very hearty thank-you to Angel Maitland for typing the supplemental financial instruments. Last but not least, I offer my heartfelt thanks to Luanda Lozano of Lozano Designs who instantly understood our intention for compiling this book as reflected in the cover motif.

Preface

------- O -------

Reality-Based Parenting: How Parents of African Descent can Cultivate Loving Relationships with their Children is offered by Center for Psychotherapy to meet the demand of African-American parents for cultural competency. Keep in mind that children of African descent, African-American, Black Parenting, and Afrikan descent are used in this book synonymously. The book is the result of feedback (parents, children, and colleagues), twenty years of critically assessing parental needs and the development of hands-on materials to supplement Center for Psychotherapy's (CFP) fifteen-week parent enrichment education classes. The subtitle of the book purports to address the unique needs of African parents in the Western world; the predominant population (98%) served at Center for Psychotherapy.

The parents we worked with are some of the most committed, passionate and responsive adults we have had the honor of serving. They have taken the Reality-Based Parenting (RBP) course and have applied it in their homes day after day, week after week, month after month, year after year; and even though many of them have made revolutionary breakthroughs, still others struggle with the paradigm. This is so because RBP is simple but not simplistic.

As a developmental and transformational process, Reality-Based Parenting is culturally specific, not universal. This is based on the multi-cultural premise of "**fullness before overflow.**" That is to say, a group must first recognize and affirm itself before it is able to share and appreciate the differences of others. Cultural competency then, is the hallmark of Reality-Based Parenting. In this book, parents are enabled to use what they have – their cultural strengths – to obtain what they want: a tested plan for nurturing children, a formula for instilling disciplining in the young, a model for psychosocial recovery.

Our ancestors bequeathed to us five vibrant legacies or strengths: the kinship bond, work orientation, adaptability, determination to succeed, and spiritual commitment. This is a minimum moral value system, without which, practice would be incorrect and possibilities would be limited as evidenced by the social mal-adaptiveness and abject servitude experienced by many people of African descent domiciled in Western societies. Our assimilation into the dominant status quo result in self-alienation and institutional disengagement, the result of the collapsing pillars of the home, school and church – institutions which have held the black family together for centuries.

Indeed, great ideals do not live on because lofty monuments commemorate their inception, nor could their inherent greatness and effectiveness alone insure their survival. Great ideals live on when and only when they become enshrined in the hearts of the young. Reality-Based Parenting is dedicated to that goal. It is aimed at helping parents transmit cultural and spiritual heritage to the next generation.

Accordingly, this offering helps parents increase understanding of their status and role in the family system. The chapters therefore are tools for helping parents to dig up the ancestral secrets so that they can be put to use. It is hoped that by developing self-awareness and acquiring self-knowledge as advocated in this book parents will be inspired to integrate its contents into their activities of daily living so that "… our sons may flourish in their youth like well-nurtured plants; and our daughters may be like cornerstones, polished after the similitude of a palace" (Psalms 144: 12-14).

Introduction

------- O -------

The continued omissions and misrepresentations of the experiences, histories, and realities of people of color in Western literature have resulted in massive spiritual alienation and institutional disengagement among too many people in the African Diaspora.

The information in this book is an attempt to fill the gap so that children of African descent could be more culturally grounded. While the heritage understanding presented herein reflects the knowledge, skills and worldview that parents of African descent need to know, other groups can benefit from the information as well.

Reality-Based Parenting is the spiritual practice of viewing or representing parent/child experiences as they really are, not as they appear, wished, or imagined to be. Moreover, RBP exists in the service of transmitting cultural and spiritual heritage to the young. Cultural competency, the distinguishing characteristic of RBP, as highlighted in this offering, refers to the development of self-awareness and the acquisition of self-knowledge.

If parents of African descent are to succeed at raising self-reliant children in our rapidly changing world, they have to adapt a different way of thinking, integrate new parenting models, internalize innovative strategies, and apply new techniques to their parenting repertoire. To these ends, RBP is dedicated. It consists of twelve separate self-contained sections assembled together for the purpose of equipping parents, guardians, and prospective parents who are interested in the goal of empowering their children with roots and wings through the development of healthy, resilient, and love-based approaches contrasted with fear-based methods.

In the immortal words of Frederick Douglas, "It is easier to build strong children than to repair broken adults." Over the years, thousands of parents have come to accept and trust our education program for its consistent, commonsensical, culturally driven, and principle-centered approaches to nurturing and building of strong children from infancy to adulthood.

This work contains some of the contents of our 15-session parent Enrichment Education program. Obviously, the actual training, which consists of groups of 12-20 parents interacting with a common purpose, is impossible to recreate with ink on paper. To have the kind of breakthrough that happens for people in our parent education classes requires being in the classes; there is no replacement. However, this book presents some to the same material that can enable you to access breakthroughs in your approach to parenting whether or not it is feasible for you to be in our support group sessions.

The value of reading the book, as in our parenting classes – and in parenting children in general – depends on your full participation and your willingness to experience something unpredictable. I therefore wish you well on this spiritual journey.

Contributing Authors

------- O -------

Love without Fear: How Parents of African Descent Can Build Effective Parent/Child Relationships

- **Shanel Jones B.S. Psychology/Kinesiology &The Health Sciences**
- **Behavioral therapist, Board Member: Family Renaissance, Inc.**
- **Brandon Jeminez B.S. Imminent, Brooklyn College**
- **Film Production, Board Member: Family Renaissance, Inc.**

Roots & Wings:

Roots & Wings: Foundations for Parenting African-American Children

(Part I)

- **Edna Jafferalli, M.A.**
  Behavioral Therapist, Practice Manager, Program Director & Leadership Training

Roots & Wings: foundations for Parenting Children of African Descent

(Part II)

- **Hermelene Thomas, BSSW, Medgar Evers College**

- **Behavioral Therapist in Practice**

Personal Parenting Philosophy

- **Norissa Williams, PhD, MSW**
- **Assistant Professor, Medgar Evers College at The City University of New York**

The Strength Perspective: Playing to Children's Strengths

- **Norissa Williams, PhD, MSW**
  Assistant Professor, Medgar Evers College at The City University of New York

The Four Parenting Styles

- **Lesa Girard, BSSW: Medgar Evers College**
- **Pauline Melchoir, BSSW: Medgar Evers College Intern Center for Psychotherapy**

The ABC's of Child Development

- **Avril Bachelor, MSW**
  Clinician, Center for Psychotherapy; Supervisor: Child Welfare Of New York

Discipline for Dignity: Rewards and Consequences

- **Tiffany Llewellyn, LMSW**
  Clinician, Family and Children's Aid

Parent/child Communication: How to Talk & Listen to Children

- **Yana Pennant LMSW**
  Clinician, Center for Psychotherapy

Learning Outside the Classroom: Transcending Artificial Boundaries

- **Nadege Waithe, MSW (Student Development Specialist) Office Assistant: Dept. of Pub. Admin & Economics, MEC**

Clinician: Center for Psychotherapy,

Parental Stress Management:

How Parents of African Heritage can cope with Stress

(Part I)

- **Elaine Reid, LCSW (Field Education Coordinator) Medgar Evers College at The City University of New York**

How African-American Parents can Manage Stress

(Part II)

- **Lorraine Oudkerk, B.S., Early Childhood Education Health and Wellness Life Coach in Practice Administrator, Center for Psychotherapy**

Co-Parenting Skills:

Co-Parenting for the Best Child Outcome

(Part I)

- **Naila Smith, MA Fordham University & Norissa Williams, MSW, PhD Medgar Evers College at CUNY**

The Father Factor: Impact of a Father's Absence

(Part II)

- **O'Neil Richards, LMSW Clinician: Center for Psychotherapy, President: OSR Consultant**

Money Management Basics: Family Economics

Money Management Basics for Parents and Children of African Descent

(Part I)

- **Ronald Richardson, Associate in Business
Certified Financial Planner & Personal Financial Analyst**

Money Management Basics for Parents of African Descent

(Part II)

- **Artis Harry, LMSW: B.S. York College, MSW Fordham University
Lincoln Hospital (NYCHHC), Clinician: Center for Psychotherapy**

About the Editor

A pioneering New York State psychotherapist since 1991, John McQueen EDS, LCSW, CFLE is the Founder/CEO of Center for Psychotherapy; an adjunctive professor at Medgar Evers College; an author, poet, and researcher who specializes in Mental Health counseling that integrates science, technology, spirituality and culture in clinical social work practice.

Love Without Fear: How Parents of African Descent Can Build Effective Relationships with Children

<u>Authors:</u>

Shanel Jones, B.S., The College of William & Mary - Psychology/Kinesiology & The Health Sciences

Brandon Jimenez, B.S. Imminent Brooklyn College graduate – Film Production

"Successful parents set their children free and become free themselves in the process."

--Anonymous

This chapter focuses on how parents can build effective relationships with children. We, Shanel and Brandon, wrote this chapter to assist parents and parents-to-be with the critical task of examining their parenting beliefs and parenting processes. After reading this chapter, it is hoped that conscientious and responsible parents will be able to identify areas in their parenting beliefs and parenting program, which may need improvement. In like manner, we hope you, the seeker, will be able to use the information in this chapter as well as the contents of this book to work toward such improvement and parent enrichment in general. In short, we wrote this chapter to enable parents in the African Diaspora to transcend fear by diving into love.

Black parents and parents to be, our liberation, which equals the success of our children, depends on, your honesty, humility, understanding, discipline and cultural fortitude. If doctors and lawyers undergo years of training before assuming their occupation, what makes you think parenting - the most important occupation in the world doesn't require same or similar, if not more training? Most parents of African descent are blamed not trained. In the eternal words of Maya Angelou, "People do what they know. When we know better, we do better." Accordingly, parents tend to be ineffective when they are not equipped with relevant parental knowledge and skills.

Keep in mind that ineffective parenting is not about blame, shame, guilt or fault. After all, we empathetically understand that a parent cannot give what he or she does not have. It is mandatory, therefore, that parents in the African Diaspora study and understand the impact of the "Maafa" (see glossary) on succeeding generations in order to fully understand why most of us parent the way we do. One thing is clear however, as parents we have to take responsibility for our thoughts and actions. Or else, all the efforts put into parenting our children for the future world will be tantamount to futility. Consider this: Why did you decide to have children in the first place? "Because the reason, for which you have children will influence their development" (*The Development of the Black Child*. YouTube video lecture, Amos Wilson).

Effective parenting is a broad topic, which relies on an understanding of many other things. So today, we begin with, "Love without fear: How Parents of African Descent can Build Effective Relationships with Children." As a parent, all of your expressions, that is your behaviors, speech patterns and thoughts emanate from one of two instincts, the life (love) instinct or the death (fear) instinct. Let us examine the death/life instinct paradigm and the purpose of the parent-child relationship.

Before establishing the death-life instinct (glossary), some food for thought: "If your black boy or black girl would have said to you twenty years ago that they wanted to be president of the United States, how many of you by being realistic would have discouraged that view? While this may have a certain realistic basis in a certain kind of a way, you are also creating the child's view of self in line with the way the society is currently structured" (*The Development of the Black Child*.

YouTube video lecture, Amos Wilson). What would have prompted the discouraging response to the child's ambition? Is it the life instinct or the death instinct? How would you use that awareness to respond appropriately to adventurous children in the future?

From the death instinct, parents operate from hate. The death instinct produces expressions of hostile aggression (beating, hitting, and or cursing at your child), disenchantment (ridiculing you child) retarding the growth of the child, restricting your child (controlling your child), and/or being ruled or controlled by fear. If you have hate in your heart, if you have anger and fear in your heart, if you have resentment in your heart, you will manifest these feelings in how you interact with your children, thus creating an environment of anger, and fear, which will create destruction in your home. (*Love & African [Black] Relationships.* YouTube video lecture, Amos Wilson, 1985). Fear plays a huge role in the death instinct because uncontrolled and unexamined fear will shut down your ability to love. Fear will make you want to control, and fear will cause you to act in a hostile manner toward our children. So if a parent operates from fear (death instinct) though they are unaware, they are actually producing damaged inferior children.

On the contrary, an effective parent realizes that social structures are created by humans, and will therefore raise their children to create the social structures needed for their advancement. Conscious parents realize that anything created by the mind of one person could be overcome by the mind of another person filled with initiative, enthusiasm and willpower. Love preserves self and others, (supporting afro-centered business, schools and health institutions); and moves towards discovery and healing (investigating what is causing the behavior in the child, rather than beating the child for not knowing how to articulate their stress). Thus, love frees parents and children from the quagmire of social oppression. Love is reconstructive; it defends, and it repairs and stimulates growth in the individual. The love instinct then is manifested when you operate in such a way as to always preserve, always nurture, always defend, always heal, always affirm, and always stimulate, develop and create a safe environment for yourself and those you love. What children experience from their parents influences how they will express their love or fear to themselves and others when they become adults. This is important because "when you have a child you don't just have a child for yourself. A child is born into a community of people, and must ultimately grow up to contribute to that community, the community's ability to support itself and its ability to protect its interest. "(*Love & African [Black] Relationships.* YouTube video lecture, Amos Wilson, 1985).

Now let us examine the term "relationship". A relationship is the commitment individuals make to each other for the purpose of developing themselves and each other into better versions of themselves. According to Cambridge Dictionary Online, the definition of the word commitment is a "willingness to give your time and energy to something that you believe in, or a promise or firm decision to do something". This means that you are loyal to the thing or person and you just can't do whatever you want or feel like.

The purpose of the parent-child relationship is for the parent and child to nurture the love instinct to exchange cultural information that leads to reciprocity, increased wisdom, understanding and responsibility of both the parent and child. Parents are also responsible for nurturing the child from infancy to adulthood so that the child is able to manage his/her own life, recognize and meet their needs, and fulfill their potential as responsible, creative and productive members of society. This exchange of information includes all communication methods: beliefs, speech, behavior; role modeling, and thoughts. Most importantly, parents must demonstrate role modeling. This is so children learn and quickly internalize what they see or experience with their parent. This exchange of information should look like figure A, not figure B.

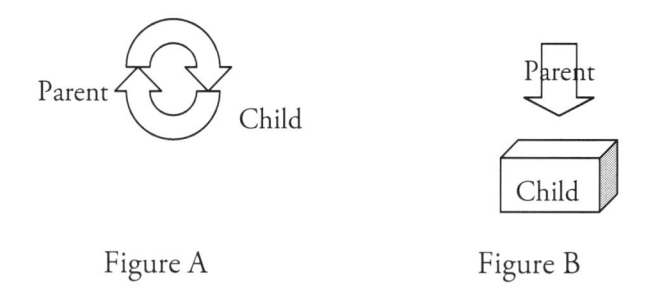

Figure A

Figure B

Note: at each exchange point in figure A, there is a level of respect, which must be maintained and not crossed or ignored in order to maintain effective communication. Meaning, being the parent does not simply allow you to speak to and touch the children in any way that you want. Parents must also respect children by showing self-control over their own speech and actions. In turn, they will be showing the child discipline as well. Some parents did not receive this respect from their parents during childhood. This is unacceptable and unfortunate. However, we need to learn quickly how to role model and demonstrate love through the act of self-control.

Effective parenting does not require the parent to pathologically "control" the child. What stops a child from engaging in behaviors harmful to themselves and others is the framework that the child operates from. This framework comprises beliefs or principles that motivate the child's thoughts and behavior. The framework includes the philosophy that the parents develops and maintains with the child. For example, "We are a Pan Africanist family. We follow the teaching of Marcus Garvey at all times". The framework must always be culturally centered; that is the beliefs and principles are based on the strengths and uniqueness of the Black family. The information you exchange with your child must be drawn from your cultural foundation.

"Culture brings order to chaos. Culture binds us to each other, it gives us identity. Culture tells us who we should live for and who we should die for. Culture is an energy source for striving; it gives us a sense of security. It also puts us into a system of accountability including being accountable to our ancestors. Culture is indeed a template for living. African culture produces Africans, African culture cultivates Africans, and no other culture can do that. So if we look at culture like this, and see it as a means by which a people protect themselves, then we can understand culture as the immune system of a people." (*What is Culture?* YouTube video lecture, Dr. Marimba Ani, 2010). This quotation is made by our African studies scholar, Dr. Marimba Ani, known for her critique of European culture and it's incompatibility with people of African descent. So you see there is great comfort in knowing your child is culturally centered, and becomes the example you the parent set for him or her.

Part of being culturally centered is having the ability to evaluate one's own connection to the world around you. In our case, Black parents must examine their connection to the White world, a relationship that influences how you will relate to your child. (*Love & African [Black] Relationships.* YouTube video lecture, Amos Wilson, 1985.) For example, if the parent believes that the European holds the standard of beauty, they will teach the child that their skin, their hair and their features are "ugly" or "bad" because it is not European. This creates low self-esteem in the child, the beginning of harmful behavior and thoughts. As the child is a reflection of the parent, parents must reflect on and develop positive behavior patterns, and thoughts. "The level of self-esteem, sense of purpose and direction of the parent is directly related to the child's performance", (Kunjufu, 1984). An educational consultant with African American images, Dr. Kunjufu observes that "effective parenting begins with the parent first." It is your role as a parent to model to your child/children, a disciplined, responsible, patient, understanding, compassionate, zealous, continually learning, and creative person. This will enable them in turn to share those qualities with other Black people around them.

Marianne Williamson once remarked, "Love is [a virtue] we were born with; fear is what we learn." We concur with Marianne that the parental journey is the spiritual act of unlearning fear and embracing love. Parents of African descent, it is instructive to know that one's approach to parenting is either fear-based or love-based; there is no middle ground.

One way to test whether or not your parenting style is love-based or fear-based is to take an objective inventory of how your discipline children. For purposes of this offering, discipline is defined as setting limits on unwanted behavior and inducing wanted behavior, which eventually becomes self-perpetuating. Our definition exemplifies the spiritual nature of discipline. It promotes the idea that as a spiritual practice discipline focuses on the inner (internal) life of children, not on their behavior. Indeed, there is a belief behind every behavior, but parents usually deal with only the behavior. Dealing with the belief behind the behavior does not mean you don't deal with the behavior. However, you are most effective when you are aware of both the behavior and the belief behind it.

Conversely, punishment or penalty inflicted on a child for an offense focuses more on the child's behavior and less on what they think or feel. In disciplining a child, therefore, one should not merely focus on the act itself (what is visible), but rather on the intent behind children's actions. In so doing, we spare children lots of pain, agony, resentment, and trauma, which often limit or inhibit their ability to thrive.

As the Bible, a book frequently referenced in the African-American community, puts it: "There is no fear in love; but perfect love casteth out fear: because fear hath torment. He that feareth is not made perfect in love." (1 John 4: 18 King James Version). According to Dictionary. com, torment means to afflict with great bodily pain or mental suffering; an instrument of torture. How does your child experience your "discipline?" Do they experience it as an act of love, a feeling of warm personal attachment or deep affection, or as an instrument of torture, extreme anguish of body or mend? An objective answer to this question will determine whether or not your parenting is love-based or fear-based.

Parents tend to parent how they were parented. Some parents often confuse discipline and punishment.. Punishment is inflicting pain or denying children of wanted pleasures. For example, typical punishments include spankings, time out, and taking sentimental objects away from children. We have vivid remembrance of some of the things our parents told us: "I am beating (spanking) you because I love you." Or "I'm taking away your toys because I have to love you into obedience or behaving well." What contradictions in a child's little mind! We were seriously confused as to how our parents (love objects) could have inflicted so much pain (fearfulness) on us. In our experience, when love and fear is convoluted like that it often results in the creation of a toxic environment for children. Keep in mind that *obedience derived from fear potentially creates the character of a rebel.*

It is believed that punishment – the way parents of African descent tend to deal harshly with their children is a derivative of chattel slavery. Their fore parents were punished by their slave masters during chattel slavery for any and all perceived "mistakes". That mode of discipline is being transmitted from generation to generation because as far as we know there have not been formal organizations or institutions designed to deconstruct the socialization of slavery and for healing the slavery wound. Hurting people hurt others. This may explain the phenomenon of punishment in the Black family.

We have an opportunity in this era to break the cycle, the generational curse, if you will, by critically examining our beliefs, thoughts and feelings about how we "discipline" our children. You are invited, therefore, to adapt the love-based instead of continuing the fear-based parenting approach, which is a legacy of slavery.

Keep in mind that punishment tends to harbor resentment in children instead of respect. This harsh reality is reflected in what experts such as Bowlby (1973, 1982, 1988), Ainsworth (1978) and others recognize as the importance of early development on children's later ability to function effectively. That caretaker-infant bonding or attachment is important in the formation of the individual. We have become increasingly aware of the value of attachment in human life. "Attachment is a deep and enduring connection established between a child and caregiver in the first several years of life. Attachment profoundly influences every component of the human condition – mind, body, emotions, relationships, and values" (Crosson-Tower, 1988).

For purposes of this chapter, we will discuss secure and insecure attachments:

> Secure attachment is best seen during normal distress when the mother, for example, leaves the child and happy enthusiasm is experienced by child when mother returns. There are two types of insecure attachment; an ambivalent (or resistant) in which the infant is clingy and upset when his or her caretaker leaves. Their response to mother's return is a mix of rejection and anger. In the avoidant type, infants stay calm when their mothers leave and respond to their return by ignoring them. It is as though infants in this category expected to be abandoned and are retaliating in kind.
>
> Bottom line, secure attachment is created through a constant, reciprocal relationship between the parent and child. Not to provide the child with such a relationship

is to compromise or disrupt this attachment and put the child at risk for a myriad of problems (Crosson-Tower, 1988).

Levy and Orlans (1998) suggest that attachment disorder can be created by circumstances and events such as parental abuse or neglect, youthful parenting, family violence, poor environmental stimulation, parental separation and even poverty.

Attachment behavior in childhood is the core or foundation for normal, healthy adult growth and development. Looking at childcare through the prism of attachment, one can see how punishment tends to negatively impact children's development. Instead, a strong bond is created over time when parents lovingly and consistently meet a child's needs. Threats communicate, what children think, feel, want or need is not important. Indeed, successful parents of African descent can set themselves free by helping their children become free through love-based opportunities for parenting effectively.

Below is a list of how parents of African descent can use the love-based approach to build effective parent/child relationships:

1. Listen more and talk less in order to focus on children's intent and less on their behavior.
2. Read More: Parents should expand their knowledge of the Maafa, the psychology of the Black child and child development. Starting with "Know thy self" by Na'im Akbar.
3. Study and be able to apply "The Black Family Pledge" by Maya Angelou
4. Turn off the "Tel-Lie-Vision": Disconnect yourself form sources of distractions that prevent you from hearing yourself, and from seeking information about yourself.
5. Practice active listening: Practice listening to children intently, not just waiting to talk.
6. Invest in building your child's self-image
7. Become unconditional love – love your child no matter what

References

Ani Marimba, Dr. (2010). *What is Culture?* YouTube video lecture

Cambridge Dictionary Online. (2014). Retrieved 12 November 2014, from http://dictionary.reference.com/

Holmes, J. (1993). *John Bowlby & Attachment Theory*. (p. 67). London, New York: Routledge.

Kunjufu, J. (1984). *Developing positive self-images and discipline in Black children*. Chicago, Ill.: African-American Images

Levy, T., & Orleans, M. (1998). *Attachment trauma & healing*. Washington, DC: Child Welfare League of America Press.

Lewis, J. (2014). *Marianne Williamson Quotes. About*. Retrieved 12 November 2014, fromhttp://womenshistory.about.com/od/quotes/a/m_williamson.htm

Pam, L. (2014). *Teaching Through Love Instead of Fear - by Pam Leo. Connectionparenting.com*. Retrieved 12 November 2014, from http://www.connectionparenting.com/parenting_articles/teaching.html

Wilson Amos, (1985). Love & African [Black] Relationships. YouTube video lecture, Amos Wilson, 1985.

Wilson, Amos, (1985). The Development of the Black Child. YouTube video lecture

Roots and Wings: Foundations For Parenting African-American Children (Part I)

<u>Author:</u>

Edna Jafferalli, M.A., Counseling & Psychology

Behavioral Therapist, Center for Psychotherapy

There are only two lasting bequests we can hope to give our children. One of these is roots, the other wings."

--Joann Wolfgang Van Goethe

Grappling with the phrase "Roots and Wings" as postulated in Wolfgang Van Goethe's quotation depicted above, one immediately conjures up images of the roots of a tree and the wings of a bird. For purposes of this chapter, however, roots of responsibility are metaphorically conceived to mean values parents instill in children that enable them (the children) to have wings of independence so that they can "rise with healing in their wings and go free, leaping with joy like calves let out to pasture." (Malachi 4:2 KJV).

In other words, roots of responsibility symbolize internalized core values that prepare children with wings to fly or soar and become great patrons to themselves, family, community, neighborhood, nation, race and world. Dr. Jawanza Kunjufu calls this sowing process "The seven levels of unity" which are taught to children of African descent in order of importance (Kunjufu, 1982). In the first of the "Seven principles of Kwanzaa," Dr. Maulana Karenga defines Umoja to mean the ability of African-American children "to strive for and maintain unity in the family, community, nation, and race." (Karenga, 1989).

Insight is a great resource parents can cultivate to help children shape and develop roots and wings for them to soar. Often times, it is children who help to create and influence parental insight. This is facilitated when parents provide a healthy emotional climate in which dialogue; collaboration, affirmation, mentorship, and authority – the central ingredients which holds relationships together – are fostered without the usual pressure.

Being a parent is a hard task. This is so because no one has a manual or clear set of rules with which they can provide the "right" nurturing, caring and structuring of children for the challenges that life often presents. Therefore, parents are challenged to develop the ability to accurately gage the potential of a child, and create the right emotional climate necessary for ensuring that this child is given the average-expectable environment to thrive. This is possibly the single most important distinction parents of African descent need to raise a strong, healthy and enduring generation. When children lack the right preparation or cultural grounding they need, their capacity to face and overcome challenges now and in future become greatly impaired. Clearly, without the right roots, the possibility of wings, flight and soaring in bright colors diminish to near nonexistence. Hence the reason for highlighting the overlapping core-components: roots of responsibility and wings of independence – a framework for developing the even more critical element of soaring.

Roots of Responsibility: The Free Dictionary defines roots as the usually underground portion of a plant that lacks buds, leaves, or nodes and serves as support. Roots draw minerals and water from the surrounding soil, and sometimes store food. As the "underground portion of a plant," plant roots constitute a metaphoric image of the grounded values that represent the foundation from which children can spring forth to fly (Dictionary, Ret. 2014).

Responsibility in this context literally means the ability to respond, not react. Value-based living is what best activates and facilitates responsible behavior in humans. People know they are responsible when their stated values and practice values are in alignment. Hence, even though the roots of a tree are not always visible, many times it is possible to determine the condition of the root system by assessing the visible parts of the tree. A very tall tree, for example, needs a very deep root system in order to maintain stability and withstand the elements. Likewise, trees with a lot of girth must have very robust root systems in order to support the mass and weight of the actual visible parts of trees. This is also true in architecture, the higher the building, the deeper and stronger its foundation. This is analogous to the important process of providing our children with root systems or value-induced responsibility, which corresponds to parents' perception of their children,'s potential.

Values are the inner moral guides for decisions as to what is right, good and true. Core values are considered to be those values that direct decisions in one's life. Examples of values are: achievement, autonomy, balance, cooperation, creativity, entrepreneurship, identity, justice, personal time, responsibility, family first, education, and health, A value meets the following criteria: (a) chosen freely (b) chosen from among alternatives (c) chosen after due reflection (d) prized and cherished (e) publicly affirmed (f) acted upon (g) part of a pattern that is a repeated action. Indeed, "When your values are clear to you, making decisions becomes easier" (Disney, 2014).

The values a child learns at a young age possibly remains with him/her all through adulthood. Values are the lenses from which children view, assimilate and interact with their environment. The right set of values help to sharpen a child's focus and form the basis for making good judgment calls. Children are constantly soaking up values from the environment like sponge in water because they are typically impressionable (Wright & Wright, 1976). It is the responsibility of the parent to first clarify their values - so that they can subsequently point out to children those values that they should retain and those that must be rejected.

The development of the right root or value system for a child is a matter of parental capability, dedication, priority, and realism. The capacity of a parent to model and provide the right root system will determine the quality of input he or she can make in the life of the child. It stands to reason therefore that deficiencies in capability be made up for by allowing input from third parties or professionals. Capability also relates to the child because as with the parents, every child is wired differently. Parents would do well, therefore, to tailor approaches to value formation or root-system development for the child to suit his/her temperament and innate abilities. The closest relative of capability is dedication. This is required for parents with adequate or less than adequate capabilities because without the right dedication, even the most brilliant people will fail. Conversely, with much dedication, it is possible for not-so-capable parents to make important achievements in parenting their child. Furthermore, dedication would drive parents to make all the sacrifices required to surround their children with the enabling environment required for excelling.

This computer age can be described as frenzied. It appears as though parents and children fall prey to many distractions. This is where prioritizing comes in - the onus is on parents to make their children's development a priority. The pursuit of wealth is believed to be one of the greatest quests of the 21st century. Sometimes this is unfortunately, at the expense of developing and modeling the right value system to our children. Some children, it is believed, learn the value of pursuing "the dollar" from a very tender age. Accordingly, they are immediately immersed into the dollar-driven culture faster than they can spell their names. In order to build the right root system, parents must consciously rank the future of their children far above all the dollars in Wall Street.

Realism is what provides the ballasts that prevent us from tipping over sometimes. In light of the fast-paced life that describes the 21st century, many times, we face the challenge of being realistic enough to know our limitations and the limitations of the children we are raising. If the "shape" of the child is such that he cannot become a sports person, it would be a waste of time and resources to build a sport-oriented value system around the child. Parents must know themselves, take assessments and determine who they truly are in light of their strengths and weaknesses. Likewise, parents must know their children, they must spend quality time studying them to discover their strengths, weaknesses and tendencies in order to structure their roots in the most adequate and effective manner (Balson, 1994).

Parenting involves nurturing, caring, providing, encouraging, nudging, affirming, correcting, educating and fortifying children until they are old enough to fend for themselves while engaging in the work of carrying on the legacy of parenting by forming new families. Contrary to what some might believe, parenting goes beyond merely providing the basics and allowing things to run amok. Indeed, parenting is a series of activities and decisions that require careful consideration and implementation. This is so because it only takes a small error to create huge emotional and psychological problems that children would carry into adulthood. Broken children become broken adults and happy children become happy adults. Furthermore, "it is easier to build strong children than to repair broken [adults]" (Douglas, Ret. 2014).

Reproduction is one major characteristic of every living organism. When viewed broadly, reproduction is not merely the process of bringing forth offspring. It also has to do with bringing forth offspring with a greater chance of survival than parents. Genetically, we are better modified than our parents and certainly better equipped to survive and thrive in our environment. It therefore stands to reason that parents should want their offspring not to merely outlive them but to have much better life experiences and life expectancies than they do. To these ends, it is expected that every parent would strive to ensure that their children are equipped to excel despite social and economic barriers. In order to ensure the survival of their children, parents must seek to provide them with deep roots or core-values that embody culture, traditions, education, confidence, justice, balance, and the right spiritual/mental attitude. They need these qualities or attributes to strengthen their wings as they launch out to soar into adulthood.

Wings of Independence: The dynamics involved in imparting wings of independence to children are almost inexhaustible, but can be narrowed down to a few critical points, some of which are often neglected by parents. They include: Values-clarification, stability, and building self-confidence. These attributes constitute wings of independence.

Like a butterfly, which undergoes profound changes from egg to lava to pupa to adult butterfly; or an eagle that lays its eggs high on the tallest trees or mountaintops completely out of reach of predators and pollutants, it is the parent's job to establish high goals for children's potential and development through their parenting philosophy and priorities. They then teach their children commensurate values and the art of value-clarification that would enable them (children) to thrive in any and all types of social conditions.

Value-clarification: An important requisite for effective functioning is the clarification of already determined personal values so that one can pursue a lifestyle in concert with them. Most of the decisions in life are based on how and why children value things. Value-clarification is the art of identifying and prioritizing values. Moreover, it is a systematic examination of values, their impact, negative or positive, on moral formation and the development of a conscience. The object of value clarification is not to teach specific values, but to make children aware of their own personally held values, to assess their lives for congruence between belief, feelings and behavior, and of the way in which their values compare to those of friends, adults, and different groups in society.

Stability: When a child is culturally grounded with the right set of values, they become the deep roots that provide the needed foundation for fairly smooth sailing through the currents of life. Parents must provide the stability needed for proper child development (Wright& Wright, 1976). Drawing one more time from the eagle's analogy: the way the parent eagle teaches its eaglets to fly is to push them off from high altitudes and catch them just before they hit the ground. This is modeled or repeated multiple times until the eaglet acquires the competency or flight stability it needs to rely on its own wings. Part of building stability and sustainability is to model responsibility to children. This is not done merely by giving them age-appropriate tasks to be completed and after having gradually mastered those tasks, proceed to ones that are more complex.

According to Dr. Haim Ginnott in "Between Parents and Child," Pg. 80: "The plain fact is that responsibility cannot be imposed. It can only grow from within, fed and directed by values absorbed at home, [in school] and in the community. If responsibility is imposed; it is often resented and resisted. The task of parents is to help children choose to be cooperative, to want to assume their share of the home duties." Stability then, is the personal value and mental attitude that children develop through modeling. It is useful for taking initiative and persevering life. When this trait is lacking, children seldom start and complete some developmental tasks.

<u>Building Confidence</u>: One of the main outcomes of value-clarification and stability is self-confidence, which is, having faith in oneself. A child requires this vital value for excellence and mastery. Self-confidence is very important when confronting challenging situations. It is essential in the education system as well because children that are more confident tend to excel better academically. Parents then must learn to help their children find their voices. In essence, children must be allowed to speak freely. This freedom of expression is one of the biggest boosts to a child's confidence. Confident children generally make great leaders because they have the right mental attitude and poise that commands the respect of others (Zimmerman & Jeffrey, 1981).

In the words of Dalai Lama, "give the ones you love wings to fly, roots to come back and reason to stay." For independents, roots and wings in this context represent legacy, sustainability of family values that determine self-determination and self-reliance. Truly, roots are great, and wings are wonderful but soaring is glorious. Soaring is tantamount to the fulfillment of one's purpose - doing what one was born to do. There is nothing more elegant than watching an offspring reach heights we had never dreamed of. This is often the payoff of proper parenting and should be the focus or intention of every parent fortunate enough to raise a child in this generation.

References

Balson, Maurice. *Becoming Better Parents. Fourth Edition.* Australian Council for Educational Research Ltd., 19 Prospect Hill Road (Private Bag 55), Camberwell,

Melbourne, Victoria 3124, Australia ($16.95, Australian). 1994. http://eric.ed.gov/?id=ED377988.

Cmhc.utexas.edu/clearinghouse/files/DP007.pdf. Accessed December 2, 2014

"Dictionary, Encyclopedia and Thesaurus - The Free Dictionary. *"TheFreeDictionary.com"*. Accessed December 2, 2014. http://www.thefreedictionary.com.

Disney, Roy E. http://www.brainyquote.com/quotes/quotes/r/royedisne183365.html. Accessed December 2, 2014.

Holden, George W., and Pamela C. Miller. "Enduring and Different: A Meta-Analysis of the Similarity in Parents' Child Rearing." *Psychological Bulletin* 125, no. 2 (1999): 223–54. doi:10.1037/0033-2909.125.2.223.

Wright, James D., and Sonia R. Wright. "Social Class and Parental Values for Children: A Partial Replication and Extension of the Kohn Thesis." *American Sociological Review* 41, no. 3 (June 1976): 527. doi:10.2307/2094258.

Zimmerman, Barry J., and Jeffrey Ringle. "Effects of Model Persistence and Statements of Confidence on Children's Self-Efficacy and Problem Solving." *Journal of Educational Psychology* 73, no. 4 (1981): 485–93. doi:10.1037/0022-0663.73.4.485.

Roots and Wings: Foundations for Parenting Children of African Descent (Part II)

<u>Author:</u>

Hermelene Thomas, BSSW Medgar Evers College

Behavioral Therapist in Private Practice

> "Good parents give their children roots and wings. Roots to know where home is, wings to fly away and exercise what's been taught them."
>
> __Jonas Salk

Parenting is a very challenging vocation that doesn't come with a manual or formal training. It is an occupation most people assume without signing up for. Hence, most parents today, it is believed, are able to accurately define what parenting is without being able to fulfill the function of the role.

So who is a parent and what credentials qualifies a person for parenting? These questions beg answers. In a random survey, twelve parents were asked the question, "What is parenting?" Each respondent gave answers that pointed to the biological nature of physically bringing a child into the world. However, while biologically bearing an offspring is in fact the act of fathering and mothering children, the term parenting refers to activity of assuming full responsibility for caring and nurturing children physically, psychologically, emotionally, socially and spiritually from infancy to adulthood. This book, and this chapter, each serve to equip African American parents with the tools necessary to be parents.

This section is captioned Roots and Wings: Foundations for Effectively Parenting African-American Children. It proposes that parents of African-American children need and deserve to have culturally-specific training and resources to help their children make effective transitions into adulthood. Bear in mind that although all children go through similar stages of development and all children need caring, nurturance and guidance, African-American children and their parents face specific challenges due to America's history of racism and its concomitants: oppression and discrimination. No doubt, the historic social, political, moral, religious and economic demands make it more difficult for African-American parents to raise confident and capable children. Few programs, if any, are designed to expressly meet the cultural needs of African-American children. This document highlights this need and seeks to fill the gaps.

Because parents of African-descent face the distinctive challenge of helping their children simultaneously cope with racism while developing and maintaining a sense of positive cultural identity, this section raises this issue and shares one parent's effort to integrate Reality-Based Parenting principles and cultural values in the education of her children. Let us therefore analyze concepts of roots and wings, literally stripping them apart, to examine their essential nature as they relate to our topic.

Roots

Webster dictionary defines roots as "parts of a plant that attach themselves to the ground for support." Roots are typically underground. They support and anchor trees. They absorb water and minerals, store energy, and produce chemicals that help to regulate growth. Roots also convey water and nourishment to the rest of the plant thorough numerous branches and fibers. Metaphorically speaking, roots represent the knowledge-base African-American children require to live, compete and succeed in the changing economy and political dynamics of the modern world. Knowledge base implies the store of information or data that is available for African-American children to draw upon.

African-American parents, therefore, are to be developmentally sensitive to the needs and challenges of their children; to the extent that they are to be able to rely on and be committed to evidence-based parental practices. If they don't understand the developmental stages of their children, their success at helping children to establish roots or values can be greatly minimized.

To understand and be able to implement the afro-centric idea as presented in this section, parents will do well to enhance their knowledge-base by studying and internalizing the enhanced version of Quassan Castro's recommendations that follow.

Twelve Tips all Educators (parents, teachers, and religious leaders, etc.) must know about educating African-American children; some of which, of course, can apply to the education of all children:

Check Stereotypes

Check any stereotypes you might have. Limiting views can result in limiting expectations of African-American children. Limiting expectations can result in limited performance. If you believe in the stereotype of the "bad boy thug," for example, you're doomed. Do not make false assumptions about your children, especially if they are contrived from [societal] negative stereotypes. If you view your child's father as a dead-beat dad or the urban school environments as a "mad" house, then guess how you directly or indirectly view your children?

Connect with your Children's Teachers

Establish a positive connection with your children's teachers from the first day of class. A phone call to show gratefulness or acknowledgment of the teacher's efforts to help your children is vital to their success and paves the way for teachers to inform you when children are struggling.

Cultural Images

Due to the overexposure to white identities in media, African American students need to see images of themselves where they are not portrayed as inferior or subordinate to whites as seen in popular culture. Read and have your children read African-American books. Hang positive images in your home and where possible in their classrooms to reinforce the beauty of African American culture. As opposed to images that consist solely of music and sports icons. Explore images from the Harlem Renaissance or photos of great Africans, African-Americans, and Caribbean heroes and sheroes-*. Select images that speak to your children, not merely images that reinforce white privilege. The conceptualization of the divine in Caucasian flesh – the God of Michelangelo's painting on the ceiling of the Sistine Chapel that permeates the imagination of many, for example, poses a challenge to children seeing themselves as being made in the image of God and embracing their own power.

Cultural Identity

Cultural identity is the acceptance of one's body, goals, cultural heritage and recognition from those who count. Know and understand the meaning of your cultural strengths. Demonstrate to the children when cultural strengths are applied in everyday life. Know your cultural strengths and the strengths and peculiarities of each child. When you've conceptualized the strengths or attributes of each child, you are saying to him or her, "I am interested in who you are, you matter and I care."

Motivation

Negative putdowns create uncooperative shutdowns. Be a motivator. Tell your children what they can do, not merely what they cannot do. Work on areas of improvement without using antagonistic language. Offer sincere praise and genuine support. Having children be involved in family meetings by way of stating positive affirmations creates a team-winning mentality and establishes family and community togetherness. Affirming and expressing positive faith in your children can also make them improve in leaps and bounds behaviorally and academically and serves to further motivate them in other areas of development.

Enthusiasm

Show your enthusiasm towards the content you teach. The love for your values, areas of interest and expertise should transmit to each and every child. Preach what you practice, versus ineffectively trying to practice what you preach. National education surveys conducted with African-American students suggest that enthusiastic educators have far greater success in the classroom. Could you fathom listening to parents, teachers and preachers who do not particularly show interest in what they teach?

After School Programs

Expose children to knowledge that is offered in after school programs that might be offered in their school or district. Identify those that are culturally-competent. Especially allow them to participate in Saturday and Sunday schools that provide supplemental cultural education. In so doing your children will have esteem boosts and will not only get to acquire knowledge riddled with high incidents of violence and crime. Instead, they will receive life-changing information. Research suggests students involved in extracurricular activities are less prone to fall prey to mischievous activity.

Value of Education and Real Life

Express the value of education. Explain the varying levels of educational possibilities one can attain. Do not assume your children know how many high school credits they need to graduate. Do not assume your students know what a bachelors, masters or doctorate program consists of. Sharing your personal journey and expectations with your children helps them to see you as a human and not just some robot with formatted instructions. Share how education connects to real life. Be bold; invite children or students to discover the works of models, great cultural thinkers, especially those in their academic areas of interest.

Forgiveness

To forgive is to let go of the need for revenge and releasing negative thoughts of bitterness and resentment. It's important for the children to know that after any challenges or misunderstanding, they do not harbor any animosity or use punishment as a weapon to "get even." Remember you are in the process of educating children, not mini adults. As parents you can provide a wonderful model for your children by forgiving. If they observe your reconciliation with family members or friends who have wronged you, perhaps they will learn not to harbor resentment over the ways in which you may have disappointed them. Truly, forgiveness is an extremely valuable life skill for children to emulate and develop.

Model Appropriate Behavior and Dress for Success

You are a role model first and foremost. Show through your actions what's considered appropriate conduct. For example, how you speak, solve problems, show commitment and interact with friends will inevitably impact your children. Also, dress for success each day you leave home. Would you trust one to lead you with sloppy or unprofessional attire? Children need to see how they will one day be required to dress as professional or responsible adults.

Suspension

Black children need viable options other than punishments. For example, children suspended from school will most likely engage in watching television or playing video games while at home on suspension. Most students view suspension as a way to take a break from school. Neither does it contribute to the academic growth of any child.

Use alternative modes of discipline, not punishment. The word discipline means to impart knowledge and skill – to teach. However, it is often equated with punishment – fear, pain and control. Always look for effective ways to set limits and instill self-control in children. For example, establish rules and if a school-aged child destroys toys, instead of replacing them, let the child learn the logical consequence: destroying toys will result in no toys to play with.

Classroom/Home-Study Format

If your child cannot sit still for long periods of time or listen to lecture formats, do not agree with the teacher to hastily send a request for special education paperwork. African American students, at times, might struggle with lecture format in grades. 6-11. African children are known to benefit from the circular approach to teaching and learning. Rather than getting information through lectures and force-fed facts and figures in the traditional vertical educational methodology, caregivers foster the engagement of each child in the learning process. Thus, students experience themselves as being teachers and learners, observers and the observed. "The traditional circular approach seeks to interpret and understand; contrasted with the conventional vertical or linear model which seeks to predict and control (Asante, 1987). If need be, teachers must allow students to get up and stretch in between instruction, or rely on small group instruction. Remember, every student does not learn instruction in the same manner. Teachers must therefore teach to students' learning styles and vary instructional methods (*Castro, 2014*).

Again, roots symbolize the knowledge-base, values, images, narratives or facts that shape children's perception of the world and their interpretation of reality. Analysis of roots highlights the importance of foundationing children in useful value systems from which unconditional love and absolute trust flow. The roots metaphor also denotes that problems cannot be addressed by concentrating on the branches or effects alone – root-cause is always the key to effective solutions.

Wings

As literal objects, wings represent rescue and protection, agility and deliberate intent, speed, strength, endurance, longevity, and immortality. Eagle's wings therefore are the perfect symbols for children's growth and development. Wings represent their ability to soar to new heights in life given their training, will-power, strength, confidence and self-determination. Like the eagle, they learn to do for themselves, their family, community, nation, race and the world.

When young eagles are learning to fly, the mother eagle, during apprenticeship, flies under them with her wings spread out to catch them if they falter. Like eaglets, human beings arrive in this world without capabilities and have to acquire them during apprenticeships. Consequently, to soar to great heights like eagles, children, like eaglets, are expected to develop transferable life skills during apprenticeships with their parents and educators.

Indeed, size does matter to the perceptive mind. It is the mammoth size of the eagle that, in part, wins its title as king of the birds in myth and lore. In spite of its enormous size, the eagle still takes flight; seemingly effortlessly. It flies high despite its strong and expansive wings. Thus, it represents a pattern of rescue, protection, agility, strength, endurance and deliberate intent.

That's why the eagle's wings are the preferred symbol for children's apprenticeships and evolution. That is, the process of growing from weak to strong, from dependent to independent, from incapable to capable. This process of habilitation prepares children for a life of excellence. This signifies how children are raised in the lifestyle and tradition of their parents. Children adapt to those traditions and develop the basic capabilities for functioning effectively within their families. The result of this on-the-job training is the relative stability, independence, and preparation that enable children to improve their lot in life.

Like an eagle that stirs up its nest and flutters over its young, spreading out its wings, catching them, bearing them on its pinions (Deuteronomy 32:11), so are good parents who are open-minded, willing, ready and able to nurture their children. Thus, they create the emotional climate necessary for helping children to be expressive during the process of developing essential skill-sets. A skill-set is a neophyte's range of skills or abilities or a particular category of life skills that are necessary for functioning effectively in the environment. These essential life skills, necessary for eaglets in learning to spread their wings, can be broken down into five basic categories as follows:

Communication skills: The skillful interpretation, expression, transmission and reception of knowledge and ideas. They enable children to communicate even negative or difficult messages without creating conflict or destroying trust.

Research and planning skills: These skills denote children's ability to search for and acquire specific knowledge through forethought. The ability to apply such knowledge, conceptualize need and develop solutions for meeting those needs.

Human technology skills: The ability to use soft skills such as interpersonal and social skills for resolving conflict, as well as relating to and helping others.

Leadership skills: The ability to organize and manage oneself in the context of family, peer groups, church, and other social groupings without being a conformist or abject follower.

Survival skills: The day-to-day skills that assist in promoting effective functioning, production and work satisfaction. This includes techniques children may use in dangerous situations (e.g. natural disasters, when stopped by the police and/or attempts to be recruited for anti-social activities) to save themselves and others.

Skill-sets inspire self-confidence, determination and courage in obedient children. The Bible puts it this way: "Children obey your parents, as you would the Lord ... honor your mother and father – this is the first commandment that promises longevity of life" (Eph. 6: 1). The reward: "They shall renew their strength; they shall mount up with wings as eagles; they shall run, and not be weary; and they shall walk, and not faint." (Isaiah 40: 31). Effective parents use expert and referent power contrasted with positional and coercive power to equip their children with the knowledge and skill-sets required for them to soar.

"Roots & Wings" in Practice

Each of the lessons pointed to in this chapter are not simply things spoken with hopes of their resulting in something positive. Conversely, each of these lessons are things I've learned along the way in my own parenting journey. As parents we often stumble—not having been handed the parenting manual we all wish we had. As a parent, I made the cardinal mistake of trying to group my two children, male and female, together under the aegis of "one family under one roof." This parenting approach was adapted from social conditioning and largely influenced by my family of origin. After becoming conversant with the universal developmental stages of children and the kinesthetic, tactile and oral learning styles of black boys, I came to realize that each child is an individual and has to be related to accordingly.

In order to evolve my parenting, I educated myself. Erikson's theory of psychosocial development (that can be found in an easy internet search), was useful in my understanding the developmental stages of my children. In particular, he described my son's stage of development as **"Fidelity:**

Identity vs. Role Confusion" (adolescence, 13–19 years). I learned that as part of normative development my son would be newly concerned with how he appeared to others. In later stages of adolescence, he would develop a sense of sexual identity. As he transitions from childhood to adulthood, he'd begin to ponder the roles he would play in the adult world. Throughout this time, he might be apt to experience some role confusion—mixed ideas and feelings about the specific ways in which they will fit into society. Understanding these issues helped me to have realistic expectations for what was happening to him, as well as it helped me to adapt my approach to best meet his developmental needs.

In addition to this--still needing to ground the understanding of my children's development in a cultural perspective—I read cultural books such as "The Conspiracy to Destroy Black Boys: Developing Positive Self-Images and Discipline in Black Children" by Jawanza Kunjufu and, "The Developmental Psychology of the Black Child" by Amos Wilson. In educating myself, my authoritarian, one-size-fits-all idea was thrown out of the window. I have since adapted new techniques that are rooted in Reality-Based Parenting plus supplemental information from Dr. Shefali Tsabary's work on Conscious Parenting. She suggests, for example, that "parents should learn simple techniques to rejuvenate parent/child connection in an effort to change destructive parenting patterns" (Tsabary, 2014). In addition, I continue to apply cultural elements such as The Seven Principles of Kwanzaa, and the wisdom with which I was raised while educating my son at home.

I have since challenged and changed the pattern of communication I have with my children, particularly with my son who is much younger (age thirteen). Instead of demanding and screaming at him to do his chores and school work, I now engage him based on the principles derived from Reality-Based Parenting: dialogue, collaboration, mentorship and affirmation. Instead of barking commands, I use techniques that enable him to take ownership of his choices. As a result, I have been noticing incremental changes in my son's attitude and behavior for the better. My new authoritative approach is gaining grounds as my son exhibits a better sense of importance and self-confidence. He is also achieving a deeper sense of cultural identity that leads to belonging, responsibility, respect, harmony and academic improvement. It is my hope that you experience the same or similar levels of transformation as you begin to apply the roots and wings metaphor to your parenting regimen.

Conclusion

Parenting is both a challenging and rewarding experience. As with any job, it requires a large set of "tools" to be effective. Parents, therefore, are encouraged to garner as much knowledge and skill-sets on parenting as possible. It's the only way children will receive the strength, the "roots", so to speak, for spiraling or soaring as high as eagles.

Imagine a tree as a metaphor for a cultural system – all the things that make up who families are. The roots of the tree are essential for the survival of the tree. They carry the nutrients needed for the growth of the tree and store nutrients for later feeding. The roots are impacted by their surroundings, and environmental factors contribute to their health and vitality. In the final analysis, my idea of "wings" is the success or attainment of a child. The spirit of freedom that was planted and anchored in the root system now makes it easy for the child to soar and spread his or her wings in life. Where those wings take them is largely dependent on the teachings and spiritual fervor that was afforded them during the formative years.

Just like the roots of a tree, cultural systems have roots that are impacted by their surroundings. A culture's rituals, traditions, ceremonies, myths, and symbols provide it with the nutrients it needs to survive. Environmental factors can change a tree uprooting it or letting it die off, making space for new life in its place. Similarly, environmental changes impact cultural systems, forcing it to adapt and change to surroundings or transition into death, creating new cultural stories that carry new life. So it is with parenting. Our children are our legacy that gives life to our eternal spirits. The deeper their roots, the stronger their wings, the stronger your spirits will survive. Indeed, "effective parents give their children roots and wings". Indeed, "Roots to know where home is and wings to fly away and exercise what's been taught to them." Herein lies the secret for helping children to metamorphose from childhood to adulthood in preparation for mastery of life.

References

Article sources: http://EzineArticles.com/49212

Parenting-boys.com. Because boys will be boys, an experienced mom of two boysshares with you her knowledge and research into the topic of boy parenting.

www.askaspeechie.com.: Helping Children Achieve Their Goals:

Parents-in-a-pickle.com Parenting children with challenging behavior is enough to drive anyone potty. This friendly, practical guide gives parents lots of tips to tame those toddlers, toddlers, tykes and teens.

Psychosocial Development, Erikson's Theory

Asante, K. (1987). *The Afrocentric Idea*. Temple University Press. Philadelphia.

Castro, Q. (2014). Twelve Tips All Educators Must Know About Educating African American and Latino Students. Retrieved form Huffington Post.

Tsabary, S. (2014). *Oprah's Life Class*. Retrieved from www.oprah.com/oprahs-life class, May, 2014.

Personal Philosophies for Parents of African Descent

Author:

Norissa Williams, PhD, MSW

Medgar Evers College at the City University of New York

"It is intent which establishes one's consequential outcomes."

T.F. Hodge

We're not often conscious of this fact, but each and every parent has a *parenting philosophy*. Parenting philosophies, also referred to as parenting beliefs, encompass the ideas parents have regarding how their child's growth and development occurs and what roles they have to play in fostering their child's growth and development (Rowe & Cassillas, 2011).These philosophies consist of values, goals and attitudes about child rearing and speak to the outcomes parents hope to achieve when interacting with their children (Hastings & Grusec, 1998). These beliefs are the framework that shapes parent-child interactions (i.e., what parents' say to children, how and when parents help children, behaviors they encourage or discourage, what they expect from their children, etc.). Such beliefs are important because they have both direct and indirect effects on children's cognitive, emotional and social development.

Consider the following two scenarios. One parent of an infant believes that children begin to walk when they are physically ready. As such, they do not play an active role in helping their child to walk as they expect it to unfold naturally. When the child begins to crawl and walk, they become actively involved at that point—praising crawling efforts, first steps and the first unassisted walk. Another parent believes you have to help infants develop their muscles in order for them to learn to walk. As such, from birth, they help their children by stretching their legs and arms in playful ways on a daily basis and also praising efforts once they actually do start walking. Do these differing parenting philosophies result in different developmental outcomes for these infants? We'll return to these scenarios momentarily to find out the differences in developmental outcomes between the two.

Where do parenting philosophies come from?

The culture and social environment in which parents are raising their children largely shapes the goals and beliefs parents have for their child's development (Rowe et al., 2011). We inevitably transmit those things within the culture that we are aligned with—while also responding to unique components of our environment. The culture and social environment also influences parenting investment strategies. Investment strategies speak to how much time parents spend fostering development in a particular area.

In general, American parents tend to have goals consistent with the larger culture. They want to have their children improve their position in life; improve their socioeconomic status and gain emotional independence. This is in contrast to what may occur in a developing country where the focus may be on physical survival and ensuring that children have food to eat. However, even though American parents tend to have the above-mentioned goals, there are subgroup differences within the culture. Some environments have unique hazards or opportunities that influence the kinds of goals parents have for their children.

We can see subgroup differences in parenting philosophies, goals and strategies when examining differences in socio-economic status and race/ethnicity. Parents in high crime areas may have goals that pertain to ensuring their children stay safe and off the street. In a study of poor, urban African American mothers this was often found to be the case (Brodsky & DeVet, 2014). However, white parents of lower socioeconomic status were also found to parent in this way (Richman & Mandura, 2013). In addition, parents of lower socioeconomic status—no matter the race/ethnicity—tend to have values of obedience and conformity (Richman et al., 2013).

As such they encourage their children to behave in the same manner—not questioning adults and authority. Children are encouraged to behave in this manner at home, school and in other contexts. There is less opportunity for trial and error or the opportunity for children to take initiative. This is not the case in middle and upper middle class contexts in which children are encouraged to be independent, think critically, question and advocate for themselves—even when they are interacting with adults. Skills fostered by parents of either socioeconomic status match their current environment, and the one in which they were raised. Obedience and conformity are adaptive in a more dangerous environment and in working class jobs, while the ability to take initiative and act independent are more adaptive in a middle class environment. As such, the strategies parents have serve both a present and future purpose.

As stated, these differences can be observed by race/ethnicity as well. Though living in the larger American context, Hill and Tyson (2008) found that African American parents also include ethnic/racial socialization practices in their parenting (i.e., teaching their children ethnic pride, and how to identify racism, as well as how to respond to it). These practices are unique to African-American parenting and are in direct response to discrimination in the American social context. The study also found that African-American parents—no matter their socioeconomic status—were more likely to encourage power and achievement than white parents of lower socioeconomic status. This could only be observed in white parenting practices when they were of a higher socioeconomic status. Each of these parenting goals results in different developmental outcomes for children.

An example of the impact parenting philosophies has on child development.

In returning to the scenarios presented earlier—in which one parent believed walking unfolded naturally and the other believed they had to help their child develop muscles to support walking—we can see clear differences in developmental outcomes. In addition, we can see cultural differences. In a study of when and how children learn to walk, white American parents are more likely to expect walking to unfold naturally, while Jamaican parents believed that children had to develop these muscles and parents were instrumental in this. Consequently, Jamaican children tended to walk months earlier than the white American children in the study.

This is not to say that one philosophy is better than the other. Decisions about which outcome is better is dependent upon the values of the individual doing the assessing. In fact, one could ask, "What's the big deal anyway? There are only a few months difference. Both children end up walking." However, this is just one example of how parenting philosophies influence development. A lot of research is available about how philosophies influence development—some positive, some negative, some much more serious than a few months difference. It is beyond the scope of this chapter to detail the many ways in which parenting philosophies impact development. It is sufficient to say that there are differences.

How can parents be more conscious of their parenting philosophies?

With knowledge that each parent has parenting philosophies, goals and strategies, one can be satisfied and merely observe their behaviors—having been empowered with a vocabulary to identify their philosophies. However, the work of parenting calls for action in addition to self-awareness. In so doing we can be intentional about the kind of growth we see in our children.

There are four general domains of development spoken about in the child development literature; social, emotion, cognitive and physical. Social development refers to how individuals act in relation to others. Emotional development relates to how well one is able to regulate their own emotions. Cognitive development relates to the development of cognitive abilities such as memory, speed of processing and comprehension. Lastly, physical development refers to growth and development that occurs in one's physical body.

If parents want to be intentional about the kind of development they are fostering in their children, they must begin by asking themselves questions like: a) what are my beliefs about how development occurs (in each of the above-mentioned domains of development) b)What do I think my role in each area is? c) What do I know or can I find out about the effects of different parenting philosophies? d) What am I doing that is good? e) What can be improved?

This chapter opened with the quote, "It is intent which establishes one's consequential outcomes." It is with "intent" that this quote was chosen as it calls for a level of consciousness on the part of parents to be thoughtful about their parenting. In responding to the everyday humdrum of life it is easy to do things robotically without much thought to the consequences of our actions. However, in parenting, we each want to optimize our child's development.

As such, the focus of this chapter is to encourage you to think about the general beliefs that you have guiding how you parent and to think about whether or not these are practices you want to continue. Some practices are handed down from generation to generation and we passively accept then though the practices no longer fit our current lifestyle. Take the time to examine these things. Writing crystallizes thought and thoughts motivate action. You are encouraged, therefore, to put your parenting philosophy in writing. Such documentation potentially crystalize your thoughts and become the gyro that motivates parenting actions.

References

Brodsky, A. E., & DeVet, K. A. (2000). 'You have to be real strong': Parenting goals and strategies of resilient, urban, African American, single mothers. *Journal of Prevention and Intervention in the Community, 20*(1-2), 159-

178. Re. from http://search.ebscohost.com/login.aspx?direct=true&db=edselc&AN=edselc.2-52.0-0033799431&site=eds-live

Hastings, P. D., & Grusec, J. E. (1998).Parenting goals as organizers of responses to parent–child disagreement. *Developmental Psychology, 34*(3), 465-479. doi:10.1037/0012-1649.34.3.465

Hill, N.E., & Tyson, D. F. (2008).Excavating culture: Ethnicity and context as predictors of parenting behavior. *Applied Developmental Science, 12(4)*. 188-197.

Richman, S. B., & Mandara, J. (2013). Do socialization goals explain differences in parental control between black and white parents? *Family Relations, 62*(4), 625-636. doi:10.1111/fare.12022

Rowe, M. L., & Casillas, A. (2011). Parental goals and talk with toddlers. *Infant & Child Development, 20*(5), 475-494. doi:10.1002/icd.709.

Playing to your Child's Strengths

Author:

Norissa Williams, PhD, MSW

Medgar Evers College at the City University of New York

"There is no such thing as being a perfect parent. Just be a real one."

– Sue Atkins

Nature versus Nurture

Nature versus Nurture is an age-old argument in the study of human development. Debates concern with whether humans are genetically programmed with certain capacities and characteristics that determine who they become, or if characteristics and capacities develop over time based on the experiences individuals have had in life. In more recent times this futile argument has been put to rest as we have come to know that both our genes (nature) and our environment (nurture) play a role in who we eventually become (Anastasi, 1958). For example, if speaking about height, it isn't that ones' genes are coded for five feet, nine inches—and that's just it—they ultimately grow to five feet and 9 inches. Rather, there is what geneticists call, *a norm of reaction* (Anastasi, 1958). As such, there is a range of potential.

The individual would have a range of possibilities—such as the potential to be anywhere from five feet, 9 inches to 6 feet—depending on what the genes say. Whether or not growth is maximized and this person reaches their full potential depends on environmental input. As such, we can see that the two (nature and nurture) go hand in hand. This means, two children could be genetically programmed the same way (i.e., a range of five nine inches to 6 feet), but have different developmental outcomes. The child who is nurtured in ways consistent with maximizing physical growth—who has a proper calcium intake and physical activity during childhood and adolescence—is more likely to reach the highest height possible.

The Relevance of Nature and Nurture to Parenting

This gem of knowledge is significant to parents for very important reasons. For one, most of our children's environmental input comes from their parents/caretakers. There are three primary ways in which parents foster their child's development. Parents shape behavior very directly through telling children what to do and what not to—"Say please and thank you,"—as well as the behaviors they praise or criticize, "Dance Jamal!" or, "Move from the front of that TV and get a book!"

They also do this by choosing to partake in some activities over others (e.g., taking your child to the basketball court, asking critical thinking questions, etc.).In essence, parents provide a context for children in which some skills or capacities are developed while others are not. Parents often choose these skills based on things they have been taught or decided are right/wrong and valuable/invaluable. Sensitive parents also do this by attuning to the strengths of their child. Nonetheless, it is important to note that the parent is very influential in whether their child reaches the maximum development possible in each domain of development. Parents should remain mindful of this fact and parent as consciously as possible.

Playing to Your Child's Strengths

Playing to your child's strengths (which is the focus of this chapter), speaks to the ability of parents to identify the strengths their children have and individualize their child's developmental experience through providing specific opportunities to further cultivate their natural abilities. Anyone that has been actively involved in the raising of children knows that no two are the same. Some strengths are obvious to all, while some strengths are not recognized as strengths at all, because they go against societal values. For example, a child that is able to articulate their point of view and defend their opinions may be viewed as disruptive or rude—whereas, this individual might be exemplifying very strong critical thinking and verbal skills.

Outside of the home context, the next most influential context of development is school. Children spend most of their time there. While this is great, as teachers, who are specialists in their content area, teach children things that parents have less specialized knowledge of—there are some pitfalls to this. Throughout American history, middle class, White America have been the main decision makers in what is learned in schools and how these things are taught. Consistent with Eurocentric values, analytic intelligence is often what is valued and fostered in most American academic institutions.

Notating of this fact is not a slight against European cultures, but points to the disconnect that may exist between the skills developed in the school context versus those developed in the Afro-centric home context. Moreover, it also points to the fact that individuals of African descent may have skills and talents not often recognized or developed in the school context. In addition, resources are limited in today's schools. As such, funds tend to be spent on the highest and lowest performing students—those in special education as well as those who are in gifted classes. The majority of children, who fall somewhere in between, don't get the same amount of attention or opportunities to develop their talents. In light of the present discussion, I am suggesting that each child is gifted—even when their gift is not traditionally recognized as, "gifted." The task of the parent is discovering and cultivating that gift.

Recent educational theorists suggest that there are different kinds of intelligence than the kind typically fostered in the school context. Howard Gardner, one of these theorists, states that we have multiple intelligences. According to Gardner there is verbal/linguistic, logical-mathematical, bodily-kinesthetic, visual/spatial, musical/rhythmic, interpersonal, intrapersonal, and naturalist intelligences (Shepard, 2004).

Verbal/linguistic intelligence is the ability to think in words and use language in a sophisticated manner to communicate complex meanings. Logical-mathematical intelligence involves the ability to perform complex mathematical operations, calculate and consider hypotheses. Bodily-kinesthetic intelligence refers to the capacity to use a variety of physical skills and manipulate objects. Visual/spatial intelligence involves the ability to think in three dimensions and use mental imagery, graphic and artistic skills. Musical/rhythmic intelligence encompasses the ability to discern pitch, rhythm, tone and timber—the ability to make music. Interpersonal intelligence speaks to the ability to understand and interact effectively with others. It involves both verbal and nonverbal communication. It requires a level of sensitivity. Intrapersonal intelligence involves the capacity to be self-aware and attuned to ones' own thoughts and feelings. It also involves the ability to use this knowledge to direct ones' life. Finally, naturalist intelligence is the ability to recognize and classify animals, plants, minerals, and animals.

There is debate in the field of educational psychology as to whether or not the intelligences outlined by Howard Gardner really represent intelligence at all, and whether the things he outlines speaks to skills or basic competencies an individual may have (Gardner, 1995). Despite these arguments, it is agreed that Gardner has broadened the understanding, identification and development of individual talents and strengths. As such, these intelligences were presented in order to get you, the parent, to start thinking of the areas in which your child is strong—so that you can begin investing time and energy in further developing these capacities. In the remaining section of this chapter, we will review ways in which parents can increase their capacity to identify, develop and maximize their child's strengths.

Identifying & Developing Your Child's Strengths

Identify your child's strengths by paying attention to what has always been true about them. Once, when my son was 2—almost 3—years old, I was driving and listening to music at what seemed a comfortable volume. At this age—not even able to articulate all he was thinking—he was bothered and said, "Mommy, please! Turn down the music. Children's are sleeping! You might wake them." He was 1) advocating for others;

2) exemplifying the ability to be empathic and take the perspective of others; 3) trying to intervene to produce more favorable outcomes for those he felt may have been slighted. Seven years later, my son says he wants to be a mayor in a city with poor people, so he can help them meet their needs. In referring to Gardner's theory, we can clearly see inter- and intra-personal intelligence. As a parent it is important to see this thread of consistency in our child's personality and keep our eyes open for opportunities to further develop it.

Identifying your child's strengths by using feedback from others. Parents get feedback from others about their child's skills all the time. Teachers have commented on whether your child is chatty, funny, quiet, friendly or artistic. You also hear these kinds of things from family, baby sitters and close friends. Pay attention to the messages you have heard and observed most frequently. Make note of these strengths. I've gotten several messages from my son's teachers on progress reports about how well he behaves with others and how important it is to my son, for him to get along with others. At present, my son excels in this area more so than he does in math or reading comprehension (where he has much more of a challenge). Although I have focused attention on making him strong where he is weak through putting him in after school programs, I am also paying attention to the refinement of his intra and interpersonal intelligence.

Educate yourself on Gardner's Multiple Intelligences. The above definitions of Gardner's Multiple Intelligences area are a brief summary over of what Gardner has classified. As a parent I encourage you to get familiar with his work. For further reading on Gardner's multiple intelligences and exercises to develop these intelligences see Shepard (2004) in the reference section. This document is short and is available for free online. In addition to this, there are a variety of other materials available online and in your local bookstore that can help you identify and develop your child's strengths. This is emphasized because we often do not have the vocabulary to identify strengths our children may have. When talents/skills go unrecognized they also go *under-developed*—or worse, *undeveloped.*

*Point out to your **children their strengths and fine-tune** them through modeling behaviors.* When you praise a child for a particular behavior they are more likely to repeat the behavior. This is more effective than criticizing or punishing a behavior, which tends to happen when we focus on weaknesses as opposed to strengths. Because this is true, parents have prime opportunities to fine tune and sculpt skills.

Another example involving my son is the fact that he is very considerate—always thinking about how everyone else will feel. Recently, his sweater was taken away in school by a teacher because he was adjusting it while walking down the hall when he was supposed to be walking in a straight line. For three weeks I coached him on asking this teacher politely to return his sweater to his classroom teacher. I praised him for considering her feelings but pointed out that in attending to her needs he was neglecting his own. Nonetheless, he didn't approach her for his sweater—fearing she would be mad at him or her feelings would be hurt. I eventually did it. While he was present I modeled for him how one could politely get their needs met and preserve the other persons feelings as well. In so doing I helped sculpt his skill. Strengths can also be weaknesses, when not well-developed.

*Be **intentional about the activities and environments** you choose for your child when considering developing their strengths.* When speaking of skills such as athletic abilities, it is easier to imagine what one has to do to encourage skill development in this area—take the child to the park or put them on a team. But what does one do when the skills are less traditional? There are always things that can be done. An introvert can be encouraged to write in a journal or write short stories. A child that exemplifies leadership abilities can be encouraged to create a local newsletter in which they coordinate many writers. Something I have done is often ask my son what he would do if he owned a restaurant and had staff or invites him to other hypothetical role-play scenarios. You can Google other alternatives as well.

Conclusion

We began this chapter with a discussion of nature vs. nurture to stimulate thought about how instrumental parents are in whether children optimize their potential. In addition to the home context, schools are an important context of development, but not a sufficient and reliable source for the development of *all* the strengths our children have. We concluded the chapter with discussions of how parents can identify and develop their child's strengths. In closing, parents are encouraged to parent as consciously as possible.

References

Anastasi, A. (1958). Heredity, environment, and the question" How?". *Psychological Review, 65*(4), 197.

Gardner, H. (1995). Reflections on multiple intelligences: Myths and messages. *Phi Delta Kappan, 77,* 200-200.

Shepard, J. S. (2005). Multiple ways of knowing: Fostering resiliency through providing opportunities for participating in learning. *Reading,* (75).

Parenting styles: A guide for Nurturing Children of African Heritage

Authors:

Lesa Girard: BSSW Medgar Evers College

Pauline Melchoir: BSSW Medgar Evers College

> A method of child-rearing is not-or should not be – a whim, a fashion or a shibboleth. It should derive from an understanding of the developing child, of his or her physical and mental equipment at any given stage, and, therefore his/her readiness at any given stage to adapt, to learn, to regulate their behavior according to parental expectations"
>
> --Selma H. Fraiberg

The American Psychological Association (APA) states that parenting practices around the world share three goals: ensuring children's health and safety, preparing children for life as productive adults, and transmitting cultural values [and spiritual heritage to the next generation] (Encyclopedia of Psychology, 2000).

The Adinkra symbol, AKOKO NAN, depicted below, is a cultural representation of what it means to be an African parent. It is formed from the hen's legs and spur. Its related proverb is "The hen treads on her chicks but she does not kill them." AKOKO NAN represents the ideal nature of parents, being both protective and corrective. It is emblematic of protection, nurture, guidance, structure and discipline; an exhortation to nurture children, but a warning not to pamper them. The AKOKO NAN symbol, which encapsulates APA's, parenting practices and which embodies the African parenting style, was developed by the Ashanti people of Ghana, West Africa, and can be traced back to the 17th century.

AKOKO NAN

AKOKO NAN

As indicated in the universal declaration of parents' functions by the APA, 2000, parenting goals around the world are basically the same. However, approaches to goal attainment may be different from culture to culture and place to place. Indeed, the way in which parents raise their children may vary in every household, culture, society, and generation. However, developmental psychologists like Diana Baumrind, Eleanor Maccoby, and John Martin, propose that there are four basic parenting styles used in raising children. These four styles are: authoritarian, authoritative, permissive, and neglectful or uninvolved parenting. These developmental psychologists have all agreed that each parenting style has different characteristics, and the type of parenting styles used to nurture children greatly affects the child's development. In this chapter, these four parenting styles are discussed in the context of raising responsible children of African heritage in an indulgent world.

First, a working definition for parenting style: according to Benson, a parenting style consists of several elements that combine to create the emotional climate in which parents communicate their attitudes and practices about childrearing. Within the context of style, parents express their attitudes towards children's responsibilities and engage in a variety of parenting practices such as administering discipline, ensuring children are doing their homework, and involvement in their children's activities. Parenting styles convey parents' overall feelings about their children through body language, temper, tone of voice, emotional displays, and quality of attention (Benson, 2010).

In other words, a parenting style is a psychological construct representing standard strategies that parents use in child rearing. The quality of parenting is more essential than the quantity of time spent with the child. For instance, a parent can spend the entire afternoon with his or her child but the parent may be engaging in a different activity and not demonstrating interest towards the child. Furthermore, a parenting style is symbolic of how parents consistently respond or react to their children. Parenting practices, then, are specific behaviors, while parenting styles represent a particular, distinctive, or characteristic manner or tone of interaction adopted in the parent/child relationship (Wikipedia, 2014).

Thus, "parenting practices are specific behaviors that parents use to socialize children, while parenting style is the emotional climate in which parents raise their children" (Wikipedia, 2014). In essence, "parenting styles are persistent patterns of behavior of a caregiver toward one or more children. They are central tendencies parents gravitate toward" (Parenting Literacy, 2014).

As indicated above, parenting styles vary from place to place, culture to culture, society to society and generation to generation. Accordingly, parents should take into consideration that no parenting style can be applied successfully to all cultures. Hence, we provide in this chapter an overview of Baumrind's parenting styles and their impact on children's development. It is intended to be a guide for science-minded parents. We believe that parents can use Baumrind's stylized model to understand how they parent, or their own parenting style. Moreover, understanding different parenting styles and their impact on children may help conscious parents navigate their tasks more effectively.

Beginning with the African axiom, "It takes a village to raise a child," many theories on different types of parenting styles have emerged over the years and the following four basic styles contributed by Diana Baumrind (1960) have stood the test of time. It gives parents a framework for understanding their own parental role and responsibilities. 'Baumrind's parenting topology,' specifically classifies the four parenting styles.

In her seminal work, Baumrind found what she considered to be basic elements that could help shape successful parenting: responsiveness versus unresponsiveness and demandingness versus undemandingness. In her research she identified three parenting styles: authoritative, authoritarian, and permissive parenting. Through the work of others such as Maccoby and Martin who expanded upon Baumrind's work, four parenting styles were subsequently established as follows.

The Authoritative Parenting Style

Benson argues that an authoritative parent exercise firm control over children, expects maturity, and institutes guidelines for children to follow. Authoritative parents also discipline the child by taking into consideration the child's needs and points of view within reason.

Parents who practice an authoritative parenting style operate with reason and control when disciplining the child. However, authoritative parents are very mindful of the discipline used or how they restrict their child's autonomy. Benson states that "authoritative parents also show warmth, love, and acceptance to their children and encourage them to be independent, autonomous, and assertive based on their own individuality" (Benson, 2010).

The Authoritarian Parenting Style

Research shows that an authoritarian parent believes in the importance of compliance, conformity, and respect for authority, parental control, and maintaining order. Those who practice an authoritarian parenting style expect complete obedience from children and will bar an action that children take to defy them. Authoritarian parents will take strict measures in punishing children if they are perceived to be defiant. The authoritarian parent often times discourage children's autonomy and instead attempt to mold children to display behaviors and attitudes that is favorable to parents. In addition, Benson argues, authoritarian strategies can stunt children's maturity by not allowing them ample experience for making decisions and taking responsibility for their own actions. He concludes that unlike authoritative parenting, where open discussions are encouraged, in authoritarian parenting, reciprocal dialog and verbal give-and-take between parent and children are discouraged (Benson, 2010).

Permissive Parenting

Permissive parents don't offer much discipline or punishment but instead they tend to be lenient and may only step in when there is a serious problem. As a result of parents choosing this method of parenting, there may be few consequences for misbehavior because parents have an attitude of "kids will be kids." Consequently, these children are usually harder to handle and are not the best behaved in public.

Permissive parents may take on more of a "friend" role rather than a "parent" role. They may encourage their children to talk with them about their problems but may not discourage a lot of inappropriate behaviors. Children who grow up with permissive parents tend to struggle academically. They may exhibit more behavioral problems and are more likely to lack respect for authority and disregard rules. They often have low self-esteem and may report persistent sadness (Benson, 2010).

Neglectful or Uninvolved Parenting

Uninvolved parents tend to be neglectful. While these parents struggle to make ends meet they end up expecting children to raise themselves. Another group of parents that fall into this category would be those who suffer from mental health issues or substance abuse problems. Teenagers have also been known to fit this group because they do not possess the knowledge base and skill-set required for negotiating developmental tasks. Accordingly, both parents and children may feel overwhelmed by life's challenges.

Uninvolved parents tend to have little knowledge of what their children are doing. They tend to establish few, if any, rules or expectations. Children may not receive any nurturing or guidance, and they lack much needed parental attention, care and supervision. When parents are uninvolved, children tend to lack self-esteem and perform poorly academically. They also exhibit frequent behavior problems and are unhappy.

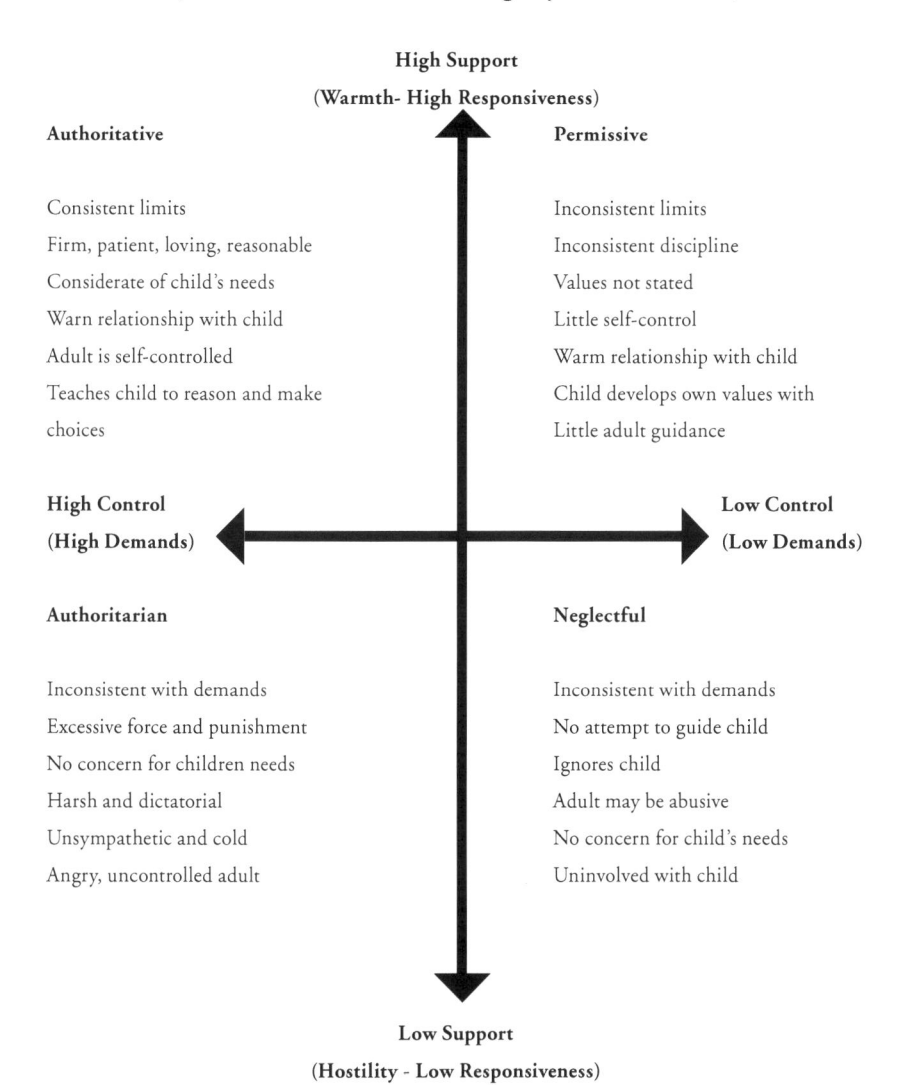

PARENT-CHILD INTERACTION
(Characteristics of Parenting Styles at a Glance)

High Support
(Warmth- High Responsiveness)

Authoritative

Consistent limits
Firm, patient, loving, reasonable
Considerate of child's needs
Warn relationship with child
Adult is self-controlled
Teaches child to reason and make choices

Permissive

Inconsistent limits
Inconsistent discipline
Values not stated
Little self-control
Warm relationship with child
Child develops own values with
Little adult guidance

High Control
(High Demands)

Low Control
(Low Demands)

Authoritarian

Inconsistent with demands
Excessive force and punishment
No concern for children needs
Harsh and dictatorial
Unsympathetic and cold
Angry, uncontrolled adult

Neglectful

Inconsistent with demands
No attempt to guide child
Ignores child
Adult may be abusive
No concern for child's needs
Uninvolved with child

Low Support
(Hostility - Low Responsiveness)

PARENT-CHILD INTERACTION
(A Quick Glance at Child Qualities in Relation to Parenting Styles)

High Support
(Warmth- High Responsiveness)

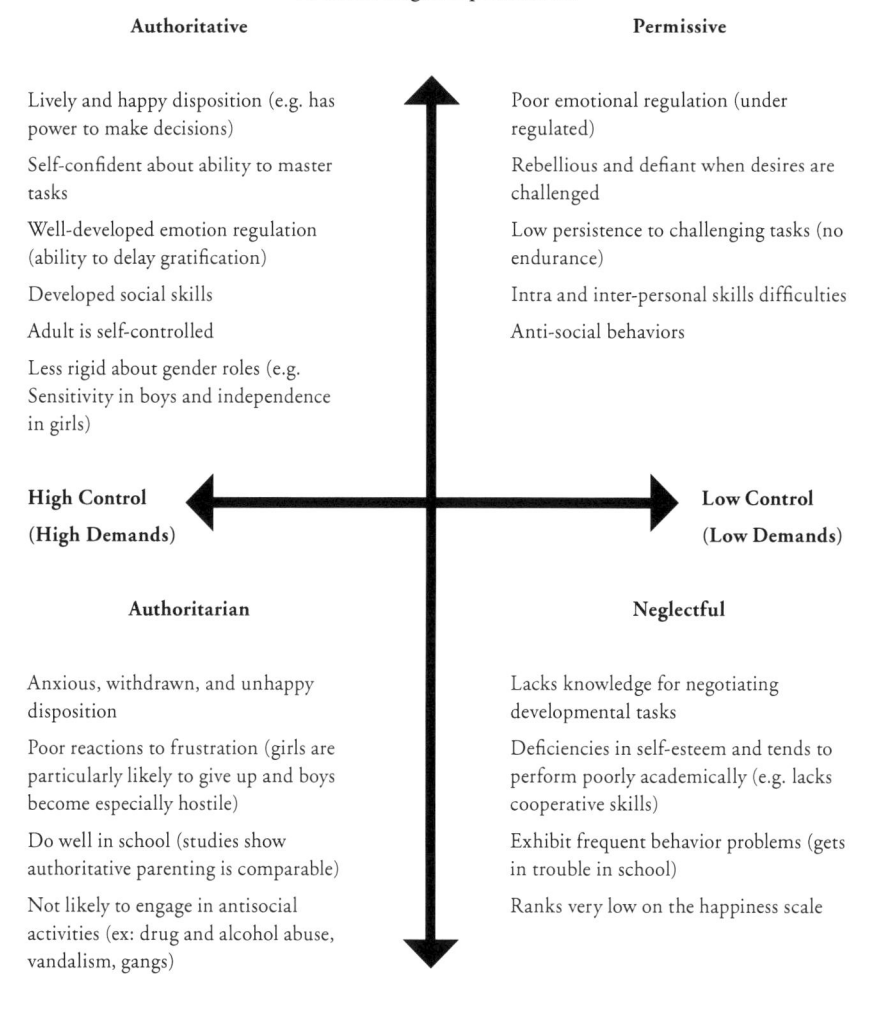

Authoritative

- Lively and happy disposition (e.g. has power to make decisions)
- Self-confident about ability to master tasks
- Well-developed emotion regulation (ability to delay gratification)
- Developed social skills
- Adult is self-controlled
- Less rigid about gender roles (e.g. Sensitivity in boys and independence in girls)

Permissive

- Poor emotional regulation (under regulated)
- Rebellious and defiant when desires are challenged
- Low persistence to challenging tasks (no endurance)
- Intra and inter-personal skills difficulties
- Anti-social behaviors

High Control (High Demands) ← → **Low Control** (Low Demands)

Authoritarian

- Anxious, withdrawn, and unhappy disposition
- Poor reactions to frustration (girls are particularly likely to give up and boys become especially hostile)
- Do well in school (studies show authoritative parenting is comparable)
- Not likely to engage in antisocial activities (ex: drug and alcohol abuse, vandalism, gangs)

Neglectful

- Lacks knowledge for negotiating developmental tasks
- Deficiencies in self-esteem and tends to perform poorly academically (e.g. lacks cooperative skills)
- Exhibit frequent behavior problems (gets in trouble in school)
- Ranks very low on the happiness scale

Low Support
(Hostility - Low Responsiveness)

So what kind of parent are you? Are you authoritative, authoritarian, permissive, or neglectful? Bear in mind that your parenting style is not an attribute that you deliberately chose. Instead, it might be an outgrowth of whose (ascribed status) and who (achieved status) you are. You do not select a style as much as it selects you. Good parenting depends on your awareness and acceptance of the way you were raised, the life you have lived and the parenting philosophy and values you consciously choose to live by. Accept and value all of who you are! The power lies in accepting who you are and what you have become, literally, what you brought into parenting. Since the largest room in the world is room for improvement, you may want to use Baumrind's parenting topology as a guide for harnessing your unique parenting practices so you can improve the emotional climate in your parent-child relationship.

Once parents have a clear understanding of the different styles, it becomes easier to define their own strategy to fit with their personal value system. As you become more and more familiar with the different types of parenting styles, you will think of yourself, what style you currently use, and what style you choose to exercise now and in the future. After a while you will begin to recognize a style in a friend or other parent you know. You will also discover that most parents are a mixture of different styles.

The literature on African descendants in the Western world has suggested that parents place great emphasis on shared parental responsibilities among community members and use physical punishment more frequently than European-American parents (Eyberg, Querido & Warner, 2014). Baumrind also found that, in contrast to her European-American sample, the authoritarian parenting style was not associated with negative behavioral outcomes, such as hostility and resistance in her African-American sample (Eyberg, Querido & Warner, 2014). Because of the ethnocentric nature of parenting styles, and because parents of African descent tend to be more authoritarian, many adult clients of African descent at Center for Psychotherapy often describe their authoritarian parents as caring, involved and concerned. They believe that their authoritarian parents modeled warmth and acceptance. They also correlate authoritarian parenting style with academic success and moral integrity. On the other hand, authoritarian parenting appears too controlling to European-American.

Keep in mind that one concomitant of the authoritarian parenting style is spanking or physical punishment. It is believed that many Black parents in the Western Hemisphere parent their children using authoritarian techniques such as spankings and denial of privileges. These are parenting strategies that were developed during the years of American slavery. According to Dr. Kerby Alvin (2014), author of "The Soulful Parent: Raising Healthy Happy and Successful African-American Children," during chattel slavery, physical punishment was functional, because whippings helped keep children safe in a racist society. Alvin's research found that African-American parents often used corporal punishment, which developed because slave masters and overseers beat slaves to keep them in line (Kerby, 2014). Physical punishment of children, therefore, may be Black parents way of insidiously perpetuating chattel slavery's negative legacies.

Now that you have a general understanding of the different parenting styles, possible source of your parenting practices, the degree to which parents are supportive and responsive to children and your parenting intention or eventual outcome of your child, you will find it easier to recognize your own parenting techniques and what can be done to achieve desired outcomes. Rather than remaining loyal or wedded to ineffective traditional parenting methodologies, for example, learn to integrate authoritative techniques in your unique parenting style in order to guide your children to a happy, successful and fulfilling life.

Baumrind, who studied parenting styles, concluded that they differ in four important areas: Parents' warmth/nurturance, discipline strategy, communication skills, and expectations of maturity. Parents are the major influence in their children's lives. Thus their perception of how children think, and should be raised is crucial in determining children's needs (Parenting Quotes, 2014). Here is a synopsis of what the studies found on the impact of each parenting style on children's development:

Authoritative parenting: this type of parenting leads to children who are successful, happy and emotionally stable; this is the preferred method. Authoritarian parenting: this type of parenting style developed obedient, respectful and academically successful children. However, they had less self-esteem, happiness, and emotional intelligence. Permissive parenting: these parents raised children who showed more delinquent behavior, had poor academic results, and low self-control. Neglectful or uninvolved parenting: The results of this type of parenting were the lowest with respect to happiness, success, self-esteem and self-regulation (Parenting Quotes, 2014).

In conclusion, Virginia Satir (1916 - 1988), a major pioneer in family therapy, summarizes the goal of this chapter in these words: "Let your children know you are human. Nurturing families … parents see themselves as empowering leaders not as authoritative bosses. They see their job primarily as one of teaching their children how to be truly human in all situations. They acknowledge to the child their poor judgment as well as their good judgment, their hurt, anger, or disappointment as well as tier joy. The behavior of these parents match what they say" (Satir, 2014). AKOKO NAN – the leg of a hen.

References

Benson, J. (2010). Parenting Styles and Their Effects. In Social and emotional development in infancy and early childhood. Amsterdam: Academic.

Encyclopedia of Psychology, <u>Parenting</u>. American Psychology Association. Washington D.C. 2000.

Eyberg, Sheila, M. Querido, June G. & Warner, Tamera, D (2014). Parenting Styles and Child Behavior in African American Families of Preschool Children. Retrieved December 31, 2014 from queridowarnereyberg2002-6-pdf

Kerby, A. Dr. (2014). The Soulful Parent: Raising Healthy, Happy and Successful African American Children. Retrieved from http://everydaylife.globalpost.com/africanamerican-parenting-techniques-1868.html

Parenting Literacy (2014).Parenting Styles overview. Retrieved December 31, 2014 from parentingliteracy.com/parenting-a-z/44-overview/47-paarenting-styles

Quotes about Parenting (2014). Retrieved from http://quotes-about-parenting .weebly.com/q

Satir, Virginia (2014). Quotes Dictionary. Retrieved from http://quotes.dictionary.vom/Let_children_know_you_are_human_its_important

Wikipedia (2014).Parenting Styles. Retrieved December 31, 2014 from http://en.m.wikipedia.org/wiki/parenting_styles

The ABC's (Awareness Behaviors Change) of Child Development

Author:

Avril Bachelor, MSW

Child Welfare Supervisor SCO Family Services

Psychotherapist, Center for Psychotherapy

Embrace your beautiful mess of a life with your child. No matter how hard it gets, do not disengage. Do something—anything—to connect with and guide your child today. Parenting is an adventure of the greatest significance. It is your legacy.

—Andy Kirchhoff

Knowledge is potential power…How many times have we heard that statement? Turns out it is true. In fact, "The more you know the less people you owe." Thus, the more you know about any situation the easier it is to handle. This is true of most situations, especially in parenting. Yes, effective parenting at its most rudimentary stage requires understanding/knowledge of your child's developmental stages. It is this knowledge that will allow you to interact with your children in a more intimate manner, thereby allowing for a more sustainable and gratifying relationship. Parents of African descent, like parents around the world want what they believe are best for their children. However, parents in different cultures may have different ideas of what is best. **Parenting** practices around the world, according to The American Psychology Encyclopedia, share three major goals: ensuring children's health and safety, preparing children for life as productive adults and transmitting cultural values. A high-quality parent-child relationship is critical for healthy development.

Developmental psychology has provided us with a vast amount of knowledge about how humans develop. It is the basis for what we know about children and the mechanism that make them tick. When trying to explain development, it is important to consider the relative contribution of both nature and nurture. Nature refers to the process of biological functions, inheritance and maturation. Nurture refers to the impact of the environment, which involves the process of learning through experiences. The notion of childhood originates in the western world and this is why the early research derives from this location. Initially developmental psychologists were interested in studying the mind of the child so that education and learning could be more relevant and effective.

There are several schools of thoughts around child development; from Sigmund Freud and his work with the Id, Ego and Superego, to Piaget and his schemas and assimilation. However the majority of theorist and experts tend to lead towards the theories developed by Erik Erickson. Erikson is also credited with being one of the originators of Ego psychology, which stressed the role of the ego as being more than a servant of the id. According to Erikson, the environment in which a child lives is crucial to providing growth, adjustment, a source of self-awareness and self-identity.

Erik Erikson (1950, 1963) does not talk about psychosexual stages, he discusses *psychosocial stages.* His ideas, though, were greatly influenced by Freud, going along with Freud's (1923) ideas about the structure and topography of personality.

However, whereas Freud was an id psychologist, Erikson was an ego psychologist. He emphasized the role of culture and society and the conflicts that can take place within the ego itself, whereas Freud emphasized the conflict between the id and the superego.

According to Erikson, the ego develops as it successfully resolves crises that are distinctly social in nature. These involve establishing a sense of trust in others, developing a sense of identity in society, and helping the next generation prepare for the future. According to the theory, successful completion of each stage results in a healthy personality and the acquisition of basic virtues. Basic virtues are characteristic strengths which the ego can use to resolve crises in later years.

Erickson has broken the stages of human development into eight (8) stages.

The ABC's of child development aims to break down these concepts and allow them to be used as tools for more effective African-American parenting. For purposes of this chapter I focus on stages 1-6. These are the stages that are involved with raising children through the pre-adult and adult years. The eight stages at a glance are presented in appendix 1. It highlights the designation, age ranges, and essential characteristics of Erikson's stages of personality development throughout the lifespan.

Babies are born with some instinctual capabilities and distinct temperaments. But they go through dramatic changes on their way to adulthood, and while growing old. According to Erikson, "each individual passes through eight developmental or psycho-social stages. Each stage is characterized by a different psychological "crisis", which must be resolved by the individual before he or she can move on in a healthy way to the next stage of development. If the person copes with a particular crisis in a maladaptive manner, the outcome will be more struggles with that issue later in life".

The Stages

Trust vs. Mistrust

Affected ages: birth-18months

During this stage infants are uncertain about the world in which they live. To resolve these feelings of uncertainty the infant looks towards their primary caregiver for stability and consistency of care. If the care the infant receives is consistent, predictable and reliable they develop a sense of trust which they will carry with them to other relationships, and they will be able to feel secure even when threatened. Inadequate, inconsistent, or maladaptive care may develop mistrust towards people and things in their environments.

Autonomy vs. shame and doubt

Affected ages: 2-3 years

Between the ages of 18 months and three years, children begin to assert their independence, by walking away from their mother, picking which toy to play with, and making choices about what they like to wear, to eat, etc. Such skills prove that the child has a growing sense of independence and autonomy. Erikson states that it is critical that parents allow their children to explore the limits of their abilities within a friendly and encouraging environment which is tolerant of failure. For example, rather than put on a child's clothes a supportive parent should have the patience to allow the child to try until he/she succeeds or ask for assistance. So, the parents need to encourage the child to become more independent whilst at the same time protecting the child so that constant failure is avoided. Over protection, feeling ashamed of behavior, or lack of support, on the other hand, may lead to too much doubt about ability to control self and environment.

Initiative vs. guilt

Affected ages: 3-5 years

During this period the primary feature involves the child regularly interacting with other children in a day-care or pre-school setting. Central to this stage is play, as it provides children with the opportunity to explore their interpersonal skills through initiating activities.

Children begin to plan activities, make up games, and initiate activities with others. If given this opportunity, children develop a sense of initiative, and feel secure in their ability to lead others and make decisions. If this tendency is squelched, either through criticism or control, children develop a sense of guilt. They may feel like a nuisance to others and will therefore remain followers, lacking in self-initiative.

Industry (competence) vs. Inferiority

Affected ages: 5-12 years

Children are at the stage (aged 5 to 12 years) where they will be learning to read and write, to do sums, to make things on their own. Teachers begin to play an important role in the child's life as they teach the child specific skills.

It is at this stage that the child's peer group will gain greater significance and will become a major source of the child's self-esteem. The child now feels the need to win approval by demonstrating specific competencies that are valued by society, and begin to develop a sense of pride in their accomplishments.

If children are encouraged and reinforced for their initiative, they begin to feel industrious and feel confident in their ability to achieve goals. If this initiative is not encouraged, if it is restricted by parents or teachers, then the child begins to feel inferior, doubting his or her own abilities and therefore may not reach his or her potential.

If the child cannot develop the specific skill they feel society is demanding (e.g. being athletic) then they may develop a sense of inferiority. Some failure may be necessary so that the child can develop some modesty. Yet again, a balance between competence and modesty is necessary. Success in this stage will lead to the virtue of **competence**.

Identity vs. role confusion

Affected ages: 12- 18years

At this stage the child's peer group will gain greater significance and will become a major source of the child's self-esteem. The child now feels the need to win approval by demonstrating specific competencies that are valued by society, and begin to develop a sense of pride in their accomplishments.

If children are encouraged and reinforced for their initiative, they begin to feel industrious and feel confident in their ability to achieve goals.

Inability to establish stability (particularly regarding sex roles and occupational choice) leads to role confusion.

Intimacy vs. isolation

Affected ages: 19-40

In this stage we explore relationships leading toward longer term commitments with someone other than a family member. Successful completion of this stage can lead to comfortable relationships and a sense of commitment, safety, and care within a relationship. Avoiding intimacy, fearing commitment and relationships can lead to isolation, loneliness, and sometimes depression. Success in this stage will lead to the virtue of love.

The years between middle childhood and early adolescence are important developmental stages that establish children's sense of identity: acceptance of body, goals and recognition from those who count. During these years, children make steps toward adulthood by becoming independent, self-aware, and involved in the world beyond their families. They come to expect they will succeed or fail at different tasks. They may develop an orientation toward achievement that will color their response to school and other challenges for many years. When adolescents are in settings (school, home, church or in community programs) that are not attuned to their needs and emerging independence, they can lose confidence in themselves and slip into negative behavior patterns such as truancy and school dropout. The hope is that if African-American parents are given the tools needed, then the idea of parenting becomes less a tug-of-war and more of a wonderful journey that will enhance all members for generations.

However, doctors Amos Wilson (Wilson, 1978) and Jawanza Kunjufu (Kunjufu, 2000), have well instructed parents of African descent that they must approach using relevant developmental theories such as Erikson's from the perspective of cultural accommodation not cultural assimilation when raising children of color. According to Dr. Wilson, "The Black child is not a white child 'painted' in black. To the Black child African heritage means something. Lack of cultural identity may lead to repression of the great potential with which the Black child is born."

The ABC's of child development is intended to orient parents in the rudiments of child maturation. It also represents a paradigm shift and behavior change in parents through the cultivation of heightened awareness. The goal is to help parents age-appropriately understand the child, the self and the situation rather than merely focusing on the behavior as were done traditionally. With this level of parental awareness, sweeping behavioral changes will occur so that "our sons may flourish in their youth like well-nurtured plants; and our daughters may be like cornerstones, polished after the similitude of a palace".

References

Aabout.Com Psychology, (2014). Erik Erikson retrieved from http://psychology.about.com/library/bl_psychosocial_summary.htm

Bieher, Robert F. and Hudson, Lynne M. (1986). Developmental Psychology An Introduction. Bostao: Houghton Mifflin Company

Kunjufu, Jawanza (2000). Developing Positive Self-Images & Discipline in Black Children. Chicago Illinois: African-American Images

McLeod, S. A. (2008). Erik Erikson. Retrieved from http://www.simplypsychology.org/Erik-Erikson.html

Wilson, Amos N. (2000). Awakening the Natural Genius of Black Children. New York: African World Infosystems

Disciplining for Dignity: Rewards and Consequences

Author:

Tiffany Llewellyn, LMSW

Clinician, Family and Children's Aid

> "Do not train a child to learn by force or harshness; but direct them to it by what amuses their minds, so that you may be better able to discover with accuracy the peculiar bent of the genius of each."
>
> **Plato**

The concept of discipline has been narrowly defined in the Western world for centuries. Hillary Clinton, in her book, "It Takes a Village," (1996) highlights the African concept of discipline, "It takes a village to raise a child." Obviously, discipline for dignity is not a new concept. However, it may be considered innovative to parents and care-givers of African descent who are seeking to know themselves while at the same time helping children to find themselves in the context of human development.

Discipline for dignity is the process of correcting anti-social behaviors through the consistent application of rewards and consequences. Aligning with Carlson (2012), effective discipline is recognizing "deviant" behaviors and keeping track of when and how often they occur. Consistent discipline must be implemented at the inception of such behaviors in order to decrease their escalation. Keep in mind that punishments do not stop negative behaviors; they reinforce them.

In this chapter, parents of African Descent are challenged to re-conceptualize their idea of what discipline is. This is in an effort to help children develop and maintain dignity and self-worth. This evidence-based practice links effective incentives and consequences to behaviors you want to see exhibited in children.

Evans, Simons, and Simons (2012) explored the influence of harsh parenting styles on African-American adolescents engaged in delinquent behavior. They sought to discover whether or not verbal abuse and corporal punishment played a role in male and female antisocial behaviors and if these two factors influenced genders differently. Three main outcomes were tested - a hostile view of relationships, emotional reactions, and low self-control. The results were astounding given that corporal punishment is still considered a normative "disciplinary" method in various cultures. It is not surprising that 30% of African-American parents interviewed reported utilizing this form of "discipline" with their children ages 13-17 years old. Corporal punishment was not the most influential in decreasing antisocial behaviors, although it appeared to influence low self-control in boys.

Bowlby (1962) postulated that behavioral and emotional problems in children surface when parents fail to provide safe and nurturing home environments for them. This theory, when used to evaluate the results of the preceding study revealed that open verbal and emotional abuse increases the likelihood of emotional reactions such as anger amongst pre-adolescent and adolescent girls and low self-control among boys. Both genders exhibited a hostile view of relationships as a result of verbal abuse by their parents. Parental hostility was also shown to foster feelings of anger and irritability, which increased the risk of delinquency in youth, leading them to engage in retaliation or revenge (Carlson, 2012).

In the following case study, Bowlby's theory is used to analyze the story of Linda and her father. This family's narrative describes how a frustrated father learned and implemented new skills to empower himself as a parent. Through applying new ethos he reaped the benefits of having the kind of relationship he longed to experience with his daughter.

Linda is a 16-year-old, African-American, adolescent female who was raised by her mother. Due to sexual abuse allegations levied against a male family friends associated with this case, Linda was removed and placed in foster care. Later, she was placed in the custody of Mr. George, her biological father. Initially, Linda presented as somber, but she was clear and concise about the goals she wanted to accomplish. Linda was referred for clinical treatment due to a series of criminal activities in which she was involved. These activities included involvement in robberies, illicit substance use, and disorderly conduct which led to her arrests.

Linda's father, a 67-year-old, African-American, male, was raised in a rigid military family. He admitted to being frustrated and hopeless due to his inability to appropriately father Linda. George used numerous approaches including some authoritarian strategies adopted from his parents to help manage Linda. Notwithstanding his efforts, Linda's behavior worsened. He had tried yelling, harsh verbal and physical punishments and withdrawal. He also considered indefinite re-institutionalization in an effort to help Linda control her behavior. Despite his best efforts, Linda continued to engage in illicit drug use, truancy from school, and she intensified associations with negative peer groups.

The result: the parent-child relationship deteriorated and negative association with the law increased. Linda grew increasingly cold and aggressive with her father. As a last resort, Mr. George requested counseling help in which he fully engaged in Dialectic Behavioral Therapy (DBT). DBT is a cognitive behavioral treatment approach that joins skills with individual therapy and phone coaching to help the client system apply skill learning in moments of crisis (Lineman Institute Behavioral Tech, 2014).

Discipline is the process of setting limits on unwanted behaviors and inducing wanted behaviors which eventually become self-perpetuating. Disciplining with dignity emphasizes empowerment of the parent as the "expert" and lead "authority" figure in the parent-child relationship. The first crucial steps, then, was to engage and obtain a thorough assessment of the client system. Mr. George was helped to see that he was in charge and therefore had the power. With a new perception of parenting and a different understanding of discipline, Mr. George embodied the principle of "beginning with the end in mind." To this end, he engaged in the development of a behavioral plan to help discipline not punish Linda. Punishment is the act of subjecting a child to pain, loss, or confinement as a penalty for an offence or fault or transgression.

The family treatment plan consisted of the following key elements: life-skills training, the value of consistency, identification and use of meaningful rewards and consequences, and increasing supports for monitoring and supervising Linda. This plan took place all in the context of cultural competency, which addresses historical and contemporary issues that are important in raising African-American children such as the impact of slavery on traditional disciplinary approaches, single parenting, child-abuse and neglect and illicit drug use.

Immediately, Mr. George pushed back. He refused to entertain the idea that he had to "bribe" Linda with gifts for her to exhibit positive behavior. Cognitive therapy sessions focused on deconstructing idolized strategies and ideas which suggest that "discipline" can only be administered through harsh treatment modalities. We also identified and assessed unrealistic expectations in the context of adolescent development. Discipline in this case represents the parent's ability to recognize, track, and decrease unwanted behavior.

During therapy with Mr. George, we identified his overarching goals and desired outcomes. We specified and detailed the behaviors he wished to see exhibited by Linda. They included an increase in Linda's attendance and punctuality at school, a decrease in substance use, elimination of criminal activities and a decrease in negative peer associations. Using a reality-based practical perspective, we weighed the pros and cons of his expectancy. For example, "Is it logical to demand that Linda go from 1-2 days of school to 5 in one week?" This led to the creation of a realistic behavioral plan for Linda. Next we developed a list of items dad noticed were meaningful to Linda. These items were used to create incentives for encouraging Linda to exhibit positive behaviors. At the same time we identified measurable ways in which Linda would be accountable for her actions if and when negative behaviors were exhibited.

We also evaluated the ways in which dad currently monitored and supervised Linda. We assessed for family supports, knowledge of peers and their whereabouts as well as collaborations with other parents and community members. Low levels of social support and poor monitoring could potentially derail or negatively alter possible results from the intervention strategies.

Consistency in implementing this plan is the hallmark by which success will be attained. We cannot expect Linda, or any adolescent for that matter, to be "perfect beings." She, too, will regress or make mistakes. Regression in her case is seen, not as failure, but as part of progression. Hence, consequences are used in the treatment plan to increase her accountability whilst helping her parent gain control and remain hopeful for the positive change in Linda. There were moments when Mr. George experienced feelings of guilt and shame regarding Linda's disorderly conduct. We were able to work through his vulnerabilities while remaining focused on the overall goal.

It is also important to note that Linda's input was incorporated into the plan of action. Her input helped to shape prioritization and translation of problems into needs and generation levels of intervention goals and objectives, and the action steps. We had agreements from all players before formalizing the contract. Linda's input facilitated our understanding of her felt needs as reflected in the beliefs behind her "misbehaviors." This process also enabled her to own the problem and remain accountable for her behavior at all times. Engaging Linda in the reinforcement of rewards component of the treatment plan is important as it symbolizes a partnership between parent and child. In so doing, the child becomes aware of parental expectations and takes responsibility for exhibiting them. Each choice of the child is personal, and the consequences do not change. This leaves the parent in an authoritative, empowered role.

Distress and tolerance skills were taught to Mr. George to assist him in regulating his emotions if and when Linda did not follow the behavior plan as specified. One goal of treatment was to help Mr.

George realistically manage feelings of frustration, hopelessness and the "wanting to give up" syndrome which in times past caused him to become verbally abusive to Linda. Mr. George was able to reflect on the sequence of events, pinpointing the moments he felt most frustrated and prone to lash out. Together, we identified interventions such as the recognition of warning signs, going for a walk or calling a friend for support. These strategies decreased stress in the moment and prohibited aggression.

Treatment of this family ended prematurely. However, before the final sessions, Mr. George reported feeling more confident in his new parenting role; he demonstrated the ability to delay gratification and his ability to regulate his emotions when frustration increased. He was able to expand his circle of support and monitoring resources. He developed and utilized community supports and was able to enlist help from parents of Linda's peers. Accordingly, Linda was able to come home each night, often informed her dad about her whereabouts, accepted responsibility for her behavior – both appropriate behaviors as well as those that were still considered "deviant" and the consequences that went with them. Linda also enjoyed the rewards received for keeping the rules she helped institute. She still engages in substance use from time to time, does not attend school every day, though her attendance and punctuality improved.

In the narrative of this single parent family are embedded numerous lessons and gems that can be generalized to parents of African descent whose methods of "discipline" are usually reflective of the legacy of chattel slavery. These parents might be in Mr. George's position in which he confused discipline with punishment, and, like him, they feel a sense of frustration and hopelessness in their roles as parents. Transferable lessons from Mr. George's story are as follows:

a) Discipline is not intended to be a painful process that leaves the parent and/or child feeling guilty, worthless, ashamed or traumatized.
b) Parenting style directly or indirectly influences the behavior of children.
c) Effective, consistent, and realistic parents can hold children accountable for their behaviors.

d) Both parents and children benefit from the implementation of natural and logical consequences
e) Your children require you most of all to love them unconditionally for who they are, not to spend your whole time trying to correct them
f) For children, dignity or self-respecting character grow with the ability to say no to oneself
g) Everything is created twice; first in the mind, and then taking appropriate action to bring these ideas into reality.
h) Rewards and consequences induce intrinsic motivation

Why is discipline important? Discipline teaches [children] to operate by principle rather than desire. "Saying no to impulses puts [them] in control of their appetites [and passion] rather than vice versa. It disposes lust and permits truth, virtue, and integrity to rule [the] mind. It was the objective of this chapter to help parents of African descent differentiate discipline and punishment and critically consider their views on discipline in the light of our definition" (MacArthur, John).

Now, reflect on the definitions of discipline and punishment. Think of your own childhood memories of discipline then resolve to heal wounded experiences. Remain open to the possibility of learning new and effective ways to manifest the results you want from your child; that is, for them to be creative, resourceful and whole. Revising your approach to discipline does not mean giving up your power and authority as the parent and expert who determines what is best for your children. Instead, disciplining for dignity is the means of co-constructing a tested and proven plan for establishing a healthy parent-child bond while experiencing the joys of parenting.

Jane Nelson summarizes the concept of disciplining for dignity as profoundly as I have ever heard, "Where did we ever get the crazy idea that in order to make children do better, first we have to make them feel worse? Think of the last time you felt humiliated or treated unfairly. Did you feel like cooperating or doing better?" Like with the example of Mr. George and his daughter Linda, when parents of African descent learn to accept children for who they are and be ever-present in their lives, their healing begins.

REFERENCES

Avery, Bill.(2105). https://www.psychologytoday.com/blog/here-there-and- everywhere/201209/30-quotes-parenting

Bowlby, J. (1969/1982). *Attachment and Loss*, Vol. I, Attachment. New York: Basic Books.

Carlson, A. (2012). *How Parents Influence Deviant Behavior among Adolescents: An Analysis of their Family Life, their Community, and their Peers. Perspectives* (University Of New Hampshire), 42-51.

Evans, S. s., Simons, L., & Simons, R. (2012).*The Effect of Corporal Punishment and Verbal Abuse on Delinquency: Mediating Mechanisms. Journal Of Youth & Adolescence, 41*(8), 1095-1110.

Heschel, Abraham Joshua.(2013).http://www.opinion-maker.org/2013/09/self-respect- dignity/

MacArthur, John. (Dec. 9, 2014). http://nlcatp.org/26-incredible-john-macarthur-quotes/

The Linehan Institute Behavioral Tech (2014). *What is DBT.* Retrieved from http://behavioraltech.org/resources/whatisdbt.cfm

Effective Communication: How to Talk so Children Will Listen and Listen, so Children Will Talk

<u>Author:</u>

Yana Pennant, LMSW

Psychotherapist, Center for Psychotherapy

> "If family communication is "good", parents can pick up the signs of stress in children and talk about it before it results in some crisis. If family communication is "bad," not only will parents be insensitive to potential crises, but the poor communication will contribute to problems in the family."
>
> **--Mary Field Belenky**

Good communication is an important parenting skill. It is very important for parents to be able to communicate openly and effectively with their children. Open and effective communication benefits not only children, but also the entire family. Parents, therefore, communicate effectively when they transmit information in an easy and natural manner. Their mode of communication facilitates the development of lasting bonds between parents and children. Indeed, one way to achieve this all-important goal of bonding is to be good communicators. In fact, research shows that relationships between parents and children are greatly improved when there is effective communication taking place.

So, what is communication really? How do parents of African descent become effective communicators? How do we, as parents, give guidance and effectively impart knowledge to children so that they listen? How do parents effectively listen to their children so that they talk?

The preceding questions are not typically considered when we interact with children. We often take for granted that when we speak to children they immediately comprehend what we say, and if they don't, we tend to assume that they are inattentive or are being defiant.

As parents, we need to challenge ourselves to pause, reflect, and think about how we communicate with children. We communicate with children to exchange or impart information, ideas, and feelings in a specific manner so that we are perfectly understood. Keep in mind, that the skill of parenting, especially effective communication, is a skill that is learnt. The rest of the chapter will highlight critical factors in parent/child communication, the implementation of which can potentially enhance the parent-child relationship.

According to the Oxford Dictionary, communication is defined as the "act of sharing or exchanging of information with someone". It seems pretty straight forward. Moss expands this definition by stating that "to be human is to communicate. Whether we realize it or not, all of us all of the time are sending messages to [and receiving messages from] children, directly or indirectly, about ourselves and them. From the way we choose to dress, to the gestures we make; from the style and choice of language we use, to the company we keep, we are all the time giving out messages to each other. Sometimes we are heard clearly; often times we are misunderstood; occasionally we get it completely wrong. The complexity and fascination of communication is part of the joy of being a parent."

Communication is, therefore, a complex process. It involves four basic steps. It involves a sender, a message, a receiver and feedback. To help us communicate effectively so that we are understood, we need to develop skills that allow us to listen, process, deliver and receive messages in a clear and concise manner.

What's culture got to do with it?

Culture has everything to do with it. Culture is defined as the shared pattern of behaviors and interactions, cognitive constructs and affective understanding that are learned through a process of socialization. These shared patterns identify the members of a cultural group while also distinguishing those of another group. Hence, parents of African descent need to know their cultural strengths (the kinship bond, work orientation, adaptation, determination to succeed and spiritual commitment) and the fact that they are defined by everything from language, religion, and cuisine to social habits, music and the arts.

In effect, culture is the spiritual foundation of parents that are bequeathed to their children. Culture is reflected in parents' attitudes, customs, beliefs and symbols. These cultural traits are transmitted through language, material objects, rituals, institutions, and art from one generation to the next. Furthermore, culture is a very important factor in how children are socialized, and therefore how parents communicate with them.

> "When parents are unable to talk to their children… they cannot easily convey to them their values, beliefs, understandings, or wisdom about how to cope with their experiences. They cannot teach them about the meaning of work, or about personal responsibility, or what it means to be a moral or ethical person in a world with too many choices and too few guideposts to follow… Talk [or conversation] is a crucial link between parents and children: It is how parents impart their cultures to their children and enable them to become the kind of men and women they want them to be. When parents lose the means for socializing and influencing their children, rifts develop and families lose the intimacy that comes from shared beliefs and understandings." (Fillmore, 1991)

The positive aspects of culture, as well as, the negative aspects of culture are also transmitted to the next generation. For instance, many parents of African heritage use corporal punishment (hitting with a switch, a belt, a shoe, or a hand; paddling, whipping, whooping, or spanking) to "discipline" their children. In reality, corporal punishment is a form of communication that sends a myriad of messages to children such as the legitimization violence as a way to solve problems, the sanctioning of repression. The instruments and language of corporal punishment may also vary, but what connects them is how often they are employed as parenting tools.

Numerous studies show negative consequences for children who are spanked, regardless of their parents' race, ethnicity, income or educational level. Children who are physically punished face higher risk of anxiety and depression, and show higher rates of aggression towards and more distant relationship with the parent, Gershoff said. Those risks are in addition to the risk of injury from parents who cross the line from a hand smack on a behind – still damaging, researchers said – to abuse that leaves children bruised or bleeding (In America, 2011).

Researchers who study corporal punishment say that parents of all ethnic groups, socioeconomic categories and educational levels practice some form of physical punishment with their children. But among the groups most likely to use it is African-Americans.

In a study Gershoff co-authored that examined 20,000 kindergartners and their parents; she found that 89% of Black parents, 79% of White parents, 80% of Hispanic parents, and 73% of Asian parents said that they spank their children (In America, 2011). But why do so many Black parents approve of "punishing" their children with spankings?

The answer to this question is complex, experts say. Some researchers have suggested it's an insidious legacy left by the brutality of slavery. Some say it's rooted in fear - that if parents don't use force to demand obedience, someone else will. Others said African-American parents, in aggregate, are disproportionately lower-income, have less education and are more likely to follow a religion that implores them not to spare the rod for fear of spoiling the child.

Corporal punishment was defined by the UN committee on the Right of the Child as:

> Any punishment in which physical force is used and intended to cause some degree of pain or discomfort, however light. Most involves hitting ('smacking', 'slapping', 'spanking' children, with the hand or an implement – a whip, stick, belt, shoe, wooden spoon, etc). But it can also involve, for example, kicking, shaking or throwing children, scratching, pinching, biting, pulling hair or boxing ears, forcing children to stay in uncomfortable positions, burning, scalding or forcing ingestion (for example washing child's mouth out with soap or forcing them to swallow hot spices). In view of the committee, corporal punishment is invariably degrading. In addition, there are other non-physical forms of punishment which are also cruel and degrading and thus incompatible with the convention. These include for example, punishment which belittles, humiliates, denigrates, scapegoats, threatens, scares or ridicules the child. (Committee on the Rights of the Child, 2007: Section 111. 11).

Many of us have been taught and continue to believe that children should be seen and not heard. This belief is often advocated by peers that are often inherited from older generations. As indicated above, many religions mistakenly reinforce the biblical imperative, "do not spare the rod and spoil the child," to justify corporal punishment. Usually some people say "*my parents beat me, see anything wrong with me? Look how* good *I* turned *out!*" Did they, really? If these "good" people allow themselves to dig deeply, they will discover through examination that spanking may have left scars (the wounded child) that they do not consciously know about.

The concept of beating as a part of communication is ingrained in some societies and passed on from one generation to the other. Again, viewed from a historical perspective, it has been argued that some of the brutality involved in corporal punishment in West Indian families can be directly linked to slavery. The slave master owned the slaves and related to them as property. Thus, slaves were subjected to spankings. As the Bible puts it in Exodus 34:7, "The sins of the fathers visit the third and fourth generations". Many families, therefore, have passed down this concept of corporal punishment from one generation to the next from chattel slavery. Powerful parents unconsciously believe that children are property and therefore do not have any rights.

If children are to be seen and not heard, when do they have a voice and when do parents begin to hear them? Based on research completed by Amber Wimstall and others, high levels of corporal punishment are related to low levels of positive communication (Wimstall, A. et al). A more authoritarian parenting style is not conducive to open parent – child communication. It is not uncommon for many parents to not talk with their children. It has not been the norm for some parents to discuss, listen, explain and encourage their children to communicate their thoughts, feelings and needs through dialogue.

According to Evans and Davis, "Caribbean parents have a difficult time communicating with their children". Some parents are unaware of the value of developing language skills, and the fact that language can be used as an instrument of thought, description and analysis. In addition, they often do not realize the importance of language in encouraging initiative-taking and creativity. Evidently, these assertions do not apply to all parents, but many, I believe, can relate to it. Times have changed and parents are now much more open, ready and willing to explore the development of different parenting skills. Contemporary parents have more access to information than in previous generations. Parents, now more than ever before have to decide if they want to discuss and explore the world with their children based on their values, beliefs and culture or if they want others to do this for them. Bear in mind that the people who communicate best with your children, will undoubtedly have the most influence on them.

Barriers to Effective Communication

One major obstacle to open communication between parents and children can be the content or subject matter. Some parents, for example, are very uncomfortable dealing with some issues such as money, sex and sexuality owing to lack of conversance or embarrassment due to deficits in their own upbringing. Some parents may be so uncomfortable with such topics that they avoid them completely. The result: they miss critical and sensitive periods for providing value-based guidance to their children. In addition, some parents may feel uncomfortable having dialogue with their children because their general mode of communicating to children is by giving directions. Because some adults never had "conversations" with their parents, they find having one with their children to be very difficult. Hearing their children express their own thoughts and ideas can be intimidating to someone who never had the opportunity to do the same during their own childhood in their family of origin. They may find the children's points of view very different and at times threatening as they struggle to understand that their children are becoming independent individuals.

The development of an effective parent - child relationship is very important for enabling children to become independent. Parents need to be open and emotionally honest about topics they may find difficult to discuss. It is okay for parents to say "This is a little uncomfortable for me, but since it is important we can talk about it" or "I am not up to date with the subject matter. Could I research the topic and discuss it tomorrow when I will be able to discuss it more intelligently?" Remember, forming an early emotional bond based on effective communication will last a life time. Build the house right with effective communication from day one.

When does communication begin?

Communication is a lifelong process. Some argue that the process begins while the child is still in the womb. Mothers have been known to instinctively rub their stomachs to sooth the unborn child. Fathers sometimes put their heads on the mother's stomach and talk to the unborn child. Music is also used to communicate effectively to neonates.

Parents communicate with the new born by the use of verbal and non-verbal cues. When the baby cries, parents attempt to identify the cause to show that they understand the child's needs. The baby mimics the sounds and facial expression of the parent, smiling back when the parent smiles, pouting when the parent pouts.

Parents continue to build on these skills by watching the baby for non-verbal cues because the baby does not have language skills. However, parents still attempt to communicate in addition to "listening" to babies. This is done so we can understand their needs and become responsive. Communication should be relevant to the developmental age of the child. For example, when we are attempting to teach safety lessons to the young child such as not touching a hot stove, we use speech, changes in voice tone, gesticulations, and role-playing. In this phase of development, parents use mostly non-verbal skills to communicate the message: "The stove is hot and you will get hurt if you touch the stove." This approach to communication is something most parents do instinctively. Without practice they use effective communication to guide and protect the child from danger and, invariably, the child listens. As the child grows older parents adapt different skills to hear and to facilitate children's hearing.

One effective way to develop communication skills is to become a good listener. This is not as simple as it seems. When we are listening we need to be present and fully engage in the process. To listen effectively, we should give children our full attention, and when appropriate, make the necessary eye contact. It is also useful to turn your body to face the children and make sure your body language says "I AM PRESENT."

In one of my therapy sessions with a father, Preston, and son, Darryl[1], Preston, worked very hard to connect with his son, Darryl, on a deep emotional level. The goal of the session was developing effective communication skills. Darryl attempted to put into practice the dialogue component of what he learned the previous week. In a communication exercise with his father, Darryl attempted to express his resentful feelings regarding his father's authoritarian style of parenting. The father sat opposite his son with his legs and hands crossed, and his feelings were masked behind what seemed like a straight, unemotional face. Preston did not nod encouragingly or express in body language "I AM PRESENT" and "I am LISTENING TO YOU." He had put up his customary unintentional emotional barrier.

---

[1] The names of all clients are pseudonyms.

When Darryl spoke, he leaned forward with his head turned to the side. No eye contact was made. He, too, had his guard up. Although the barrier that existed in the parent-child relationship was invisible, initially, it became visible or real to them through exploration. We also discovered that the father was unconsciously aloof. His aloofness was not deliberate as he was fully engaged in counseling sessions and wanted to be there for his son. However, his body language was not conducive to open and effective communication. He eventually learned how to be present and use listening, hearing, and emotional intelligence skills.

If parents sincerely wish to communicate with their children so that they will listen, and listen so that they will talk, they should start modeling active listening by showing interest in what is being said to them by children and others. It is not developmentally healthy to believe that children should only listen to the parents. We may not like or agree with what is being said at times. However, communication is a two way process. At home, parents should give children undivided attention when communicating, especially when discussing difficult topics. This approach may be difficult initially, but it is an effective way to engage children.

It is often useful for parents to convey a sense of importance to the child being spoken to by talking with them quietly in private, away from other children. Convey information with a smile, and encourage expression with a nod. Does your posture say "I am open, ready and willing to listen? Relax even if you prefer not to hear what the child is saying. If you disagree with what's being said, do not become judgmental. Do not listen with a ready-made answer. Instead, listen attentively until the child is finished. Yes, you may inject a few questions for clarity and understanding but do not dominate the conversation. Remember it is a dialogue not a monologue. It is also important to understand the meaning of the slang that your child may be using. Get clarification if you do not understand a term. You can paraphrase what was said this way: "I think you said … Is that correct?" or "do you mean …" This is to ensure that you fully understand the thoughts and feeling your child wants to convey to you. Use the opportunity to connect with your child.

Effective communication really starts at an early age. Always talk with your children and explore ideas about life in an age appropriate way.

Values may remain the same but rules will change as the child grows older. Communicate with clarity what rules are nonnegotiable and which ones are flexible based on the age of the child. Instill the idea from an early age that no topic is taboo. This will encourage the child, and they are more likely to talk to you on any subject-matter. You do not have to agree with everything that your child tells you and you should stand firm on what is morally right especially if you believe their position deviates from family norms or may be dangerous. Remember that the children, especially the young adults, are exploring new ideas and values. Parents should explore their own feelings about sensitivity topics and not use their own discomfort to make a topic taboo.

Open communication must be established and maintained at an early age. Take the first step and let your child know that you are open to communicate with them. Create the emotional climate that will make communication easy. Know your child; talk about school and interact with their friends. Use news items and current affair topics to stimulate conversation. Get involved with children's interests. Find out what the values are of the people they spend time with. Discuss your expectation and continue to explore values. If the child engages you in a difficult subject do not be judgmental. Instead, communicate your views, values and belief in a non- judgmental way. If they choose to come to you it is because they value your opinion. If you start the conversation using negative words, the likelihood is that the child may not trust you enough to come back and talk to you again.

Communicate your thoughts, values and beliefs to your children when they are at an early age. Continuing to do so as they grow will strengthen your parent-child relationship. Being a bully and insisting that you are right will not be effective. Let effective and open communication be the norm in your family.

Effective communication

Effective communication builds better relationships. It allows for better understanding of the person and the situation being talked about. It also builds a trusting and caring relationship. It is in these types of environments that children tend to develop critical thinking and problem-solving skills. The way adults react to their children is the way that children will see themselves. The negative or demeaning words used to describe them, such as "you're rude", "he is so bad", "you do not listen", "he lies all the time", once communicated shapes the type of child he or she is becoming. So, moving forward, use only positive, affirming and meaningful words to communicate with children - words that are uplifting and inspirational spoken to them in non-critical ways. Tell them that you love them, check-in on them, find out how they are feeling. In short, communicate unconditional love to them. If you plant the seed for positive communication for now and the future, everything will flow in the divine order as expressed in the words of Kahlil Gibran in the poem "On Children".

References

Clarke, C. (2011) *Tout Mon Caribbean Journal of Cultural Studies: In a Fine Castle.* Childhood in Caribbean Image/Nations. Corporal Punishment in Trinidad: A Dilemma of Childhood Discipline. Vol 1: No.1 August 2011

Fillmore, Wong, L. (1991). *When Learning a Second Language Means Losing the First.* Early Childhood Research Quarterly, 6, 323-346.

In America (2011). Retrieved from: http://inamerica.blogs.cnn.com/2011/11/10/researchers-african-americans-most-likely-to-use-physical-punishment/

Louis, H. (2004). *You Can Heal Your Life.* Hay House. Indiana

Moss, B. (2008). *Communication Skills for Health and Social Care.* London, Sage.

Nichols, M. (1995).*The lost Art of Listening.* The Guildford Press, New York

Oxford Dictionary (2014). Retrieved from: http://www.oxforddictionaries.com/words/the-oxford-english-dictionary

Smith, D. E., Mosby, G. (2003). *Jamaica Child-rearing Practices: The Role of Corporal Punishment.* Free Online Library.

Kahil Gibran (2014) *The Prophet* (hard cover). One world Publishers, Massachusetts.

Learning Outside the Classroom: Transcending Artificial Boundaries

Author:

Nadege Waithe, MSW (Student Development Specialist)

Clinician, Center for Psychotherapy

> "Because schools suffocate children's hunger to learn, learning appears to be difficult and we assume that children must be externally motivated to do it. As a society, we must own up to the damage we do to our children…in our families and in our schools. We must also be willing to make the sweeping changes in our institutions, public policies and personal lives that are necessary to reverse that harm to our children and to our society."
>
> ~ Wendy Priesnitz

"Must we always teach our children with books? Let them look at the mountains and the stars up above. Let them look at the beauty of the waters and the trees and flowers on earth. They will then begin to think and to think is the beginning of a real education" (Polis, 2014).

According to *Webster's New Universal Unabridged Dictionary,* "learning" means: knowledge acquired by systematic study in any field of scholarly work or the act or process of acquiring knowledge or skill. However, when we put the word 'learning' in the context of our topic "*Learning*

Outside the Classroom," it means to use places other than the classroom for teaching and learning. Well, what does this mean to the Black family?

First, keep in mind that as important as school is, it is not the only setting where children can learn. Children do not only need to have notebooks, book bags, white boards, and quizzes to learn. True learning isn't just about memorizing facts and figures. Learning is an interactive and lifelong process of analyzing, questioning, synthesizing and discussing. Learning is looking for new meanings and unique applications of knowledge in every situation.

It is important for parents of Afrikan descent to know that there is a big world of questions, places, and people in the out of doors. Expose your children to as many meaningful experiences as possible. Experience will broaden their knowledge, harness their childhood and cultivate the type of awareness and appreciation that cannot be taught from a textbook.

Second, let us look at our school systems. Our children spend most of their time in school so there is a level of expectation that all of their learning is done within those walls. Rarely do we find primary educational institution welcome the idea of students questioning information being given to them. So what happens to all their questions? What happens when the children get home? How do children expand on what they learn away from the rigidity of the classroom?

Father and daughter, Mr. Jacob and Nichole[2] voluntarily came to Center for Psychotherapy for counseling help. Nichole is a 16-year-old young lady of Afrikan decent. Her parents were born in American; so were the rest of her family including her great, great grandparents. Nichole's parents were married until she was eleven years of age. Since then, according to her father, both mother and father have been co-parenting in order to provide the best upbringing for her and the rest of their children. Nichole is the younger of two children. Her brother is 19 years of age and is away in college.

According to her father, Mr. Jacob, Nichole was brought up in an intellectually stimulating environment. However, in recent time she has

---

[2] The names of all clients are pseudonyms.

demonstrated a lack of motivation in academics. Her father believed that Nichole needed some additional guidance and welcomed supplemental support.

Nichole's assessment indicates that she agreed with her father's conception of her situation. She admitted that she was not motivated to do any academic work. She explained that the conditions of the school along with changes in the teaching faculty distracted her. Nichole admitted that she used the separation of her parents as an excuse for not getting her school work done. She explained that she needed something to distract her father from his focus on her failing grades and therefore used her parents' separation. Therefore, the separation of her parents was ruled out as a contributory factor for lack of interest in school. As a result, we focused on the role of the school setting.

Nichole was disinterested in academics because she felt that she could not relate to the content of the subjects being taught. Some parents might not care whether or not their children can relate to the information being taught. They just want their children to produce: do the work, pass the class and graduate from school. Unfortunately, Nichole's parents fit into that category. Despite this setback, Nichole wanted to know the real purpose for learning core academic components and what they would do to enhance her learning as well as her life.

When Nichole was asked what she wanted to do when she grew up, she did not know how to answer the question. At the time of pre-engagement, her interests included watching television, hanging out with friends, and internet face-time. Strangely enough, her father explained that he and Ms. Peters[3], her mother exposed her to an intellectually stimulating environment and supported her in anything she wanted to do. However, Nichole apparently showed no interest in anything positive, particularly in academics. Remaining mindful of this fact, another goal of treatment was to help Nichole's mother and father to parent Nichole as consciously as possible.

With respect to the second goal, Nichole's parents were both given chapters two and four from this book: '*Roots & Wings: Foundations for*

---

[3] Ms. Peters is a pseudonym for Nichole's mother.

Effective Parenting' and *'The Strength Perspective: Playing to the Child's Strengths'*, to read as home assignments. According to Dr. Williams in The Strength Perspective, "it is important to note that the parent is very influential in whether their child reaches the maximum development possible in each domain of development. Parents should remain mindful of this fact, and parent as consciously as possible."

According to Dr. Williams, the goal of this assignment is to have Nichole's parents to identify their child's strengths by paying attention to what has always been true about her. By assigning these chapters, I hoped that Nichole's parents would come to realize that growing children have a natural tendency to become interested and curious about the various complexities that make up this world. Therefore, they would see that they have been focusing on their undesired activities (Nichole's involvement with TV, friends and internet face) rather than consciously focusing on her strengths. When parents focus on children's strengths, they are able to engage them in stimulating and activities that further enhance their strengths as well as turn weakness into strengths.

In the subsequent therapeutic session, both mother and father came to therapy. This I perceived to be a good sign of therapeutic engagement as the father was able to get his wife to do the homework assignment as well as attend therapy sessions. When asked if they knew their daughter's interests, they admitted that they were unaware before completing the assignment. Now they recognize Nichole's interest in wanting to help people. They believed, however, that their daughter never showed much interest in anything. When Nichole's interest in wanting to help people was emphasized, they mentioned that her interests are good, but she needs to motivate herself.

Nichole's parents expect her to be highly motivated. I inquired of them how well did they prepare Nichole to be self-motivated when she was growing up as a child. The mother stated that she would take her daughter on trips outside of New York to expose her to places outside of her 10-block radius. While engaging in these trips were well-intentioned, how much of them were deliberately educational? It is clear from my interviews and perceptions of Nichole and her parents that she was never taught the virtues of self-knowledge. Specifically, who and whose she was and what she was all about including the purpose and meaning of her present existence and the next phase or passage in her life. Nichole's education lacked knowledge of self as a person and as a child of Afrikan descent living in the Western world.

Nichole's education was abstract and pretty much confined to the walls of her school and whatever home assignments she was given. A child who probably was not positively motivated growing up would have a difficult time becoming self-motivated. Nichole's parents wanted her to be inspired, yet Nichole did not have the cultural foundation - the spiritual ethos that forms the frame of reference on how to be motivated. Accordingly, she emulated her cousin who decided to elevate her grades during the last year of high school.

Ms. Peters reported that she has plans to take Nichole on vacation out of state. I recommended that she take Nichole on a very famous tour in Washington consisting of Afrikan-American exhibits, museums and other places of interest. These suggestions excited as well as sparked a discussion with Nichole in the discussion about learning outside of the classroom. Nichole appeared excited at the thought of visiting places of interest to children of African descent. Accordingly, she entered into an agreement with her mother that when they take vacation, they would create a family outing to incorporate a visit to the suggested places. It was my assessment that if Nichole had supplemental education outside of the classroom walls, she would have a better understanding of who and whose she is, where she wants to go in life and a better view of herself as an intellectual Black young lady.

In the ensuing sessions, we discussed the educational value of Nichole's cultural-educational trip to Washington which included trips to museums and other places of interest to Nichole including the Afrikan-American Burial Ground in Manhattan. When it seemed appropriate, I eventually asked Nichole what she believed is her purpose in life as a young lady of Afrikan descent. Although she could not give meaningful answers to these questions, she became curious about existential issues. She asked questions about God, the Bible and Egyptians as well as other historical and Biblical events. Nichole's eyes appeared to sparkle and a light bulb appeared to have been switch on in her brain when conversations about self-knowledge were discussed. Nichole appeared to be fascinated by this new information that was never taught in her history classes. This interest helps to explain Nichole's lack of motivation and her inability to relate to subjects in school.

According to UNESCO (2014), "providing students with high quality learning activities in relevant situations beyond the walls of the classroom is vital for helping students appreciate their first hand experiences from a variety of different perspectives. Experiences outside the classroom also enhance learning by providing students with opportunities to practice skills of enquiry, values analysis and clarification and problem solving in everyday situations". This became evident with my sessions with Nichole.

I could sense that Nichole was starting to think differently about herself and the world around her. Despite having these insightful sessions, Nichole was still unable to connect learning in the classroom to what it meant for her future other than getting "a good job". When asked why she was not performing at her optimal, she always gave an answer that showed how uninspired she was about learning and unsure about where her life was heading. As a young lady of color who was on the verge of entering her third year in high school, Nichole had no sense of who she was and what she wanted to do with her life.

I began to explore with Nichole to see what she observes on a daily basis that could be something she could pursue as career. After a lengthy pause, she realized that she would really like to help people who are sick. She admired the swiftness and resourcefulness of first responders. When asked if she has ever volunteered, she had no knowledge that she was able to do so. Hence, discussions ensued about possible high school internships she may apply for in her area of her interest.

Toward the middle phase of treatment, it seemed that Nichole's parents lost interest in psychotherapy, and Nichole got side tracked. Unfortunately, they did not return to therapy despite outreach promises made by her father to return to treatment. Given the insight Nichole gained in our initial work together, I believe that with self-knowledge the right tools and education outside of the classroom, Nichole's interest in learning would have been stimulated and natural curiosity about self and the world would have been restored.

It is clear from Nichole's situation, that self-knowledge is truly the foundation of all true knowledge. It appears also that many parents do not understand the importance of engaging children in learning outside of the classroom. It seems as though once children outgrow the school age (6 – 12 years), parents believe that the school is supposed to facilitate the whole learning experience. They tend to forget that children (regardless of age) are forever inquisitive, curious and adventurous.

I believe with The Counsel for Learning Outside the Classroom (CLOTC) that "every child, whatever their age, ability or circumstances, should be given the opportunity to experience life's lessons beyond the classroom walls as a regular part of growing up…These experiences expand the horizon of children and young people, thus opening their eyes to the wonders of areas such as art, heritage, culture, adventure and the natural world" (CLOTC, 2014).

Afrikan people in the Western world do not have the luxury of learning about their history in classrooms since they were not allowed to build these institutions. School systems therefore give our children, if anything, limited and distorted details, if not lies, about who and whose they really are. It is the job of parents to make sure that their children receive the education they are not receiving in the classrooms as reflected in Nichole's case. Because she didn't know herself, she was unable to relate academics to her life and living in the inner city. The consequence: she had no intrinsic motivation. "Parents need to build institutions … so that four hundred years later their descendants can say, 'That's what they left'" (Na'im Akbar, Acts of Faith). Parents need to equip themselves with the knowledge and the skills necessary to supplement their children's schooling so that they will be able to make clear connections between self and world. We need to tap into their strengths to enhance the skills that they appear to be weak in.

In the final analysis, if we are to truly educate present and future generations, if we are to truly give our children roots and wings as advocated in chapter two of this book, we must encourage learning outside the classroom. Following are a list from Parents.com of seven ways to improve childhood education outside the classroom: recognize the value of the public library, explore the world at every opportunity, embrace everyday education, get a dose of culture, have some faith, take every opportunity to answer "why?", get plugged into technology -- but do it wisely (Parents.com, 2014). At home, questions should always be welcomed and not stifled. Healthy curiosity should always be encouraged and not suppressed. Learning should be a life-long process.

My experience working with teenagers has taught me a very important lesson: children who are more exposed to nature, the arts, music, and their own culture are more academically inclined and tend to be better able to make useful connections, between self and the world. They are ultimately more realistic, culturally inclined and more rational. I believe, now more than ever before, that all children and young people of African heritage should be provided with a range of experiences outside the classroom, throughout their educational journey. "I imagine a school system that recognizes learning is natural, that a love of learning is normal, and that real learning is passionate learning. A school curriculum that values questions above answers…creativity above fact regurgitation…individuality above conformity and excellence above standardized performance….. And we must reject all notions of 'reform' that serve up more of the same: more testing, more 'standards', more uniformity, more conformity, more bureaucracy" (Peter, 2014).

References

Akbar, Na'im. *Acts of Faith*. By Iyanla Vanzant. (1993). New York. A Fireside Book.

(CLOTC, 2014). *Learning Outside the Classroom*. Retrieved from http://blog.gaiam.com/quotes/authors/david-polis/8156

Parents.com (2014). *Parents and learning*. Retrieved from parents.com/kids/education/7-ways- to-educate-your-children-outside-the- classroom/

Peter, Tom. (2014). *Learning outside the Classroom*. Retrieved from : www.tompeters.com

Polis, David. (2014). The Art of Learning. Retrieved from http://blog.gaiam.com/quotes/authors/david-polis/8156

UNESCO, 2014). *High Quality Learning*. Retrieved from: http://www.unesco.org/education

Webster's New Universal Unabridged Dictionary (1996), Second Edition of *The Random House Dictionary of the English Language*. (1996). Learning. New York: Barnes & Noble Books.

How Parents of African Heritage Can Cope with Stress (Part I)

Author:

Elaine E. Reid, LCSW (Field Education Coordinator)

Medgar Evers College at the City University of New York

> Parenting in general tends to bring on stress ... being a single parent, though, is twice the work, twice the stress and twice the tears but it is also twice the hugs, twice the love and twice the pride.
>
> --unknown

Many would argue that parenting begins when one's offspring is in-utero. This, for sure can be a joyous life event. We know, however, that the one thing that is missing after giving birth to an innocent and magnificent new born, is a parenting manual. Hence, the dictum "parenting is a life-long learning process". Along with the child's negotiation of developmental tasks and accomplishments of developmental milestones come many joyous moments and equally as many challenges. Accordingly, the parenting years, as implied in the quotation above, can be an especially stressful period of life. At least part of the reason may be so many important decisions about changes in lifestyle are usually packed between the life stages of expansion (parental beginnings and subsequent years) and contraction (eventual separation of youth).

The big question is: What can a parent do to manage the demands that are invariably a part of parenting? Much of what is said in other chapters of this book should help parents manage their parental roles, career choices, financial worries, other family problems and the like. But there is more to be said. A great deal of stress reduction comes from identifying sources of stress and learning healthy strategies for coping with them. This chapter is dedicated to that goal.

What is stress, anyway? We tend to think of stress as wear and tear on the human body. Accordingly, almost any activity may produce stress. However, it is the accumulation of certain kinds of experiences that takes the greatest toll on the body. Common reasons for stress are a conflict-ridden rapidly changing and hurried life-style. Anything that causes an adverse bodily reaction is a stressor. For example, stress may derive from many changes in a person's life or a too hurried pace (Williams & Long, 1983). Another way of defining stress is the state of tension and anxiety produced by severe or prolonged frustration (Evans & Smith, 1970).

There are many theories concerning stress. Each contributes to our understanding of it. Yet, none of them answers all the questions. What follows is a case example of how one family used specific therapeutic strategies to cope with an especially stressful facet of parental life. It is hoped that the chapter would help you, the reader, to pay attention to areas of stress in your life. Most importantly, we hope it will sensitize parents to the fact that stressful experiences not only deplete your physical resources but may do so in a non-restorative fashion. Also, the physical toll stress takes on the human body is cumulative and while parents can do something to slow the accumulation, restoring what they have lost may not be possible. Therefore, the earlier they learn to prevent and reduce stress, the less they will lose physically.

Client's background/personal history

The following is the case of 'Norma[4],' an attractive 32 year old African American female who looks younger than her stated age. Norma migrated from the English-speaking Caribbean to the United States

---

[4] All names are pseudonyms

while in her early twenties. She is a college graduate who is employed as an administrative assistant at a major financial institution. Norma stated that her assimilation to the "American Culture" was very challenging due to the fact that most of her early development was spent in the English-speaking Caribbean.

Norma found it challenging to break away from the Caribbean tradition in which the parental role was rooted in authoritarianism contrasted with what appeared to her to be parental permissiveness as practiced in the United States, in which parenting roles are less restrictive. This conflict is typical of households in which parents are of African descent.

Presenting problem

Norma is a single parent with two sons, ages 14 and 6 years old respectively. She contacted the agency for consultation because she was "at her wits end" and did not know what to do about her 14 year old son 'Trevor'. She was forthcoming with information during the intake and became tearful at times during the interview process. She gave account of her son's behavior, her struggles to make ends meet, and wanting the best for her sons.

Norma stated that Trevor was coming home late from school, his grades were steadily declining and when she spoke to him about the changes in his behavior he was very disrespectful. At one time he remarked, she said, "I can't wait to be age 18 to get out of here." Norma reported that she noticed changes in his behavior when he commenced high school. Norma reported being an insomniac or being awake at nights just "thinking about what can happen to Trevor when he is away from home." As a result, she found it difficult to concentrate at work, and had feelings of hopelessness and helplessness because of her inability to effectively communicate with Trevor.

Norma also reported feeling restricted in her ability to discipline Trevor due to her fear of the State's involvement through (Administration for Children's Services), and being put in a position where her parental rights might be threatened. One of her major concerns was that she did not want her son to become a "statistic" like many young African American males. Given her environmental experiences, she was aware of many incidences in which young, Black males were targets of police brutality. Also, she thought of how young Black males can be influenced by their peers and other insidious environmental entrapments in their effort to "fit in". Still another of her concerns was that she did not want her 6 year old to mimic his older brother's negative behavior. Even with having access to a support system in the form of her mother and sister, Norma bore the burden alone. She made a decision to withhold information about Trevor and what's happening in her nuclear family from her extended family because she felt it was her responsibility and not theirs.

Initial assessment of the client's situation

The initial assessment revealed that Norma was overwhelmed by feelings of hopelessness and helplessness as a result of not being able to effectively communicate with Trevor. Norma's concern about what seems like Trevor's inappropriate behavior resulted in her inability to concentrate at work. This led to worry about the possibility of jeopardizing her job and ultimately her family's wellbeing. This is especially so since her employment was her only source of income. Norma expressed feelings of isolation and being emotionally drained because she felt compelled to cope with her situation alone because of the non-involvement of her children's father whose whereabouts are unknown, and she resisted burdening the members of her support system.

A major source of Norma's stress emanated from the difference in disciplinary approaches in her culture of origin contrasted with those practiced in her adopted culture. Her experience of growing up in the English-speaking Caribbean informed her parent-child interaction in clearly defined roles in which children were expected to respect their elders and obey their parents "in the Lord" or be subjected to some form of punishment. According to Norma, "the two disciplinary methods are very different". Hence, she felt restricted in disciplining or reprimanding Trevor in an effort to keep him in line with her parental values.

Summary of therapeutic sessions

Using task analysis (the process of breaking down the goal for any broad undertaking into its constituent parts in order to proceed in a step-by-step fashion toward the realization of the goal), therapy sessions focused on: (a) exploration of the concept of adaptation i.e. dealing with the validity of both cultures including her psychological concerns of adjusting to a new culture; feelings lost, culture shock and separation from her motherland, family and friends. This also included discussions about appropriate and acceptable methods of discipline and the impact of father's absence (b) exploration of Eric Erickson's Psychosocial Stages of Development to help Norma make possible connections between her son's "disrespectful" behavior and its relation to his phase of development (c) assessment, development and prioritization of personal and family goals; (d) to have Trevor be included in Norma's therapy sessions to address parent-child conflict. Below are the four most important goals that Norma felt she needed to work on in order to reduce or relieve parental stress.

Goal 1: Norma will define the concept of adaptation as a verb (i.e. adaptation as a process of evolution) and a noun (adaptation as a product of evolution) to help her see the merits of making healthy adjustments from motherland to adopted or transplanted land. Client will also define and understand the value of human change (autoplasticity and alloplasticity) in the context of migration that potentially contributes to stress.

Goal 2: Norma & Trevor in individual sessions will analyze and synthesize Erikson's model of psychosocial development to help them become familiar with the phase-appropriate developmental tasks of adolescence and the model's application to Trevor's behavior and lifestyle.

Goal 3: Norma will develop new strategies for helping Trevor by using the therapeutic process to improve parent-child communication and, ultimately, resolve their parent-child conflict.

Goal 4: Norma & Trevor in joint therapy sessions will develop communication skills for improving lines of communication and eventual resolution of parent-child conflict.

The following is a synopsis of what transpired over the next fifteen sessions between Norma and her son, Trevor:

Norma expressed in the previous session her skepticism about talking with Trevor about participating in psychotherapy with her due to his resistance and the stigma associated with mental health. Despite dialogues and role plays used to prepare Norma for engaging Trevor in dialogue about participating in the next and subsequent joint therapeutic sessions, she reported that her son was reluctant to attend therapy sessions because "nothing was wrong" with him. She therefore needed help on how to encourage him to participate in therapeutic sessions with her.

The therapist contacted Trevor and after using engagement skills of support, universalization, encouragement, and reaching out Trevor reluctantly agreed to attend one session. Prior to conducting joint therapy sessions, an initial one-to-one session was held with Trevor in order to build rapport and offer some reassurance that the therapeutic environment is a sacred space that teenagers found to be safe, confidential and useful for sharing their feelings, aspirations and concerns by themselves and with their parents.

During the first session Trevor told his mother a) he felt she doesn't care about them (him and his younger sibling) anymore because she hardly spends time with them; b) she comes home late from work and on the weekends; she is busy taking care of household responsibilities; c), he felt she was not listening to him when he spoke to her; and d) the reason he comes home late from school because he stays back after class to get assistance with his homework.

Norma tearfully explained to her son the reason for working late when the opportunity arises in an effort to have money to pay the bills and provide for their needs because she does not want them to be lacking for anything. She also expressed that she is fully aware of not being able to spend enough quality time with them, not because she does not love them, but because she is busy working in order to provide for them.

She also communicated her fears about his safety when he is not at home. She said she is afraid of him becoming a target of the police as well as drug and gang recruiters who are always on the prowl, desperately trying to recruit prospective young Black males who they perceive to be vulnerable.

Trevor too, started crying and apologized for being "disrespectful" to Norma at times. He also shared his mistaken beliefs that "she did not care about him anymore."

Norma reassured Trevor that she loves him and his brother very much. She was proud that he is in high school and was confident his grades would improve and that he would graduate on time. This meeting set the stage for identifying targeted behaviors (actions Norma & Trevor perceived as needing to change with individual self-management and family planning). Changes in these behaviors were worked on in subsequent sessions as reflected below.

Profound change in client-system?

During therapy sessions, Norma and Trevor had the cathartic experience of ventilating. They were able to verbalize utterances or expressions of ideas, fears, opinions, and complaints, feelings, and past significant events, along with moments of connection. The result of this ventilation was release of anxiety and tension resulting in improved functioning. For example, Norma gained a better understanding into her son's developmental needs (identity versus role confusion) and how those needs might have played a role in Trevor's perceived "misbehavior". Trevor gained some insight into his mother's intention of caring for the family's wellbeing, such as, her reason for working overtime when the opportunity presented itself. Accordingly, Norma and Trevor developed a plan for maintaining gains made in treatment. The plan included:

I. Norma will spend more quality time with Trevor alone, i.e., they will go to the movies, bowling or participate in an activity of his choice within reason on the last Saturday evening of each month.

II. Trevor promised to get all school work done in a timely manner and complete household chores, i.e., wash the dishes, make his bed each morning and help with cleaning on Saturdays. In addition, he will call to inform his mother if or when he is required to remain for afterschool class to get homework assistance. He also reassured his mother of his desire to succeed in life and that he is not, nor will ever be involved in gang or any other illegal activity, he added "I am determined to make you feel proud of me, ma."

Take away from former stress-inflicted client system

1. Regardless of your motherly and fatherly responsibilities, always reserve dedicated time for your children. Choose to spend quality time with them. Quality time makes them feel loved, wanted and cared for. It sends the message that they matter.
2. Create an emotional climate that facilitates self-expression or emotional honesty, especially around issues of father absence and school activities. This mode of operation prevents children from being stuck in the trauma triangle (see glossary for meaning)
3. Parents must age-appropriately share their life stories, needs and concerns with children. As seen in our case example, children will be mindful of parent's needs and challenges and willingly cooperate. It is obedience without content that generates resentment and resistance.
4. For successful acculturation, immigrants must learn how to integrate cultural practices of their original homeland with those of their new or adoptive home. Adaptation is a useful and vital life skill immigrant families need to master. Applying integrative skills has the potential for minimizing frustration, anger and the sense of hopelessness and helplessness transplanted spouses, parents, youth and children generally experience (Edwards, 1991).
5. It is important for parents to become familiar with Eric Erikson's epigenetic model of the developmental stages of children (Biehler & Hudson, 1986). Research indicates that children undergo a number of developmental adjustments including biological, cognitive, emotional, spiritual, and social changes. Parenting effectively in any developmental period requires understanding these normative developmental changes.
6. Don't overwhelm yourself buy fretting about your entire situation. Handle each issue as it comes, or selectively deal with matters by way of prioritization.
7. Seek help from an agency that provides culturally sensitive family support and counseling services.

Managing stress

Stress includes mental, social and physical symptoms such as exhaustion, loss of or increased appetite, headaches, crying, sleeplessness or oversleeping. Escape through alcohol, drugs, or other destructive behavior are often indicators of stress. Feelings of alarm, frustration, or apathy may accompany stress. Stress management is the ability to cope with situations, people and events that make excessive demands on the body. Managing stress is all about taking charge of your thoughts, emotions, schedule, and the way you solve problems. You can make a new start by studying and establishing stress buffers (busters) as prescribed in the NEW START acronym that follows:

N   Nutrition: (see USDA food guidelines in appendix 3)
E   Exercise: (American Heart Association guidelines in appendix 3)
W   Water: (7 – 8 glasses per day)
S   Sunlight: (The body requires vitamin D3. Get significant amount of sun exposure required to meet vitamin D requirements).
T   Tenacity of Spirit: (The process of finding meaning and connections with self and significant others and having the determination to embrace all that makes life worth living even in the face of overwhelming odds).
A   Air: (Avoid exposure to air pollutants. Avoid shallow breathing, take ten deep breaths every day).
R   Rest: (get enough sleep. Take time to be in the moment, rest your body and renew your spirit. Done well, it promises to be the best vacation you have ever taken).
T   Temperance: (Temperance is abstinence of that which is harmful and moderation of that which is healthy. Restraint, control and balance of the elements in NEW START)

Parental frustration and conflict are impossible to avoid. Stress is usually the result. Learning how to handle stress begins at birth and continues through life. The indecision and unpleasant emotions generated by stress increase tension and anxiety. These negative emotions continue to develop until some satisfactory means to the blocked goal is found.

Remember, severe and prolonged stress can lead to serious physical (heart disease and ulcers) as well as emotional and mental illnesses.

It is of utmost importance therefore that parents address challenges as they arise. More often than not, adults feel that children are not mindful of the challenges they are experiencing, when in fact, they are well aware that something is amiss. Therefore, adults, trust your instincts and communicate age-appropriately with your children. Let them know you are experiencing some challenges but it does not alter your love for them. As evident in our case example, take action and improve the quality of your life and those of your children.

References

Biehler, Robert F and Hudson, Lynn M (1968). <u>Developmental Psychology</u>. Houghton Mifflin Company. Boston.

Edwards, Haskell, G. (1991). <u>The Immigrant Family</u>. We Care Associates. Canada.

Evans, Idella M. and Smith, Patricia A. (1970). <u>Psychology for a Changing World</u>. John Wiley and Sons, Inc. New York.

Long, James D & Williams, Robert, L. <u>(1983)</u>. <u>Toward a Self-Managed Lifestyle,</u> Houghton Mifflin Company. Illinois.

How African-American Parents Can Manage Stress (Part II)

<u>Author:</u>

Lorraine Oudkerk BS, Early Childhood Education

Health & Wellness Life Coach in Practice

> **Stress is the trash of modern life – all [parents] generate it but if they don't dispose of it properly, it will pile up and overtake their lives.**
>
> **—Danzae Pace**

As implied in the preceding quotation, parental stress is an inevitable aspect of parenting. Whether you are a stay-at-home parent or a working parent, a single parent or a married parent, parent of one child or several children, stress is unavoidable. Parental stress is defined by Kirby Deater-Deckard "as a normal part of the parenting experience" (Kirby, 2013). It arises when parenting demands exceed the expected and actual resources available to parents that permit them to succeed in their role.

Being a parent is considered to be one of the most important jobs in the world. This job is inherently full of joy and satisfaction. However, it is also one of the hardest and most challenging vocations (Byrne, 2013). Parenting is described as one of the most challenging vocations because parents are charged with the responsibility of shaping their children in a way that promotes success, and helps them to function more effectively in society. Thus, parents shape the future of the world because they shape the children.

Within families of African descent the task of parenting is even more complex. The duties of parents may be further multiplied when they must be performed within very demanding situations and with limited personal and physical resources. This maybe the case for some African-American parents who tend to fall into the lowest social strata and continue to experience disparities in areas of health, education, and wealth (Jones, 2010).

Along with the enormous financial responsibilities it takes to nurture a child, African-American families are usually subjected to race-related challenges that further complicate child rearing. These challenges may place supplementary demands on African-American parents and potentially trigger additional stress (Jones, 2010).

As children grow, discipline becomes another source of stress. In addition, there is the misconception that parenting stress ends when the child reaches a certain age. This, and other incorrect assumptions, often contributes to parenting being more stressed than it has to be. Often this condition leads to adrenal fatigue and a collection of physical symptoms.

The stress you feel as a parent, therefore, will continue throughout the course of your life and the life of your children. The sources of stress (whether it is separation, divorce, finances, child-care, racism, arguments or a combination of two or more stressors), and how best to manage them, is what changes as you and your children grow. Stress-free parenting is as much of a myth as Bigfoot. Stress is an inherent aspect of parenting; you cannot eliminate it. However, you can prevent some stress and effectively manage the rest. Needless to say that unhealthy stress is bad for health and negatively affects parenting. According to Christine Carter, parents' ability to manage their own stress is the second most powerful predictor of their [children's] well-being; of love and affection (Carter, 2011).

Following are four techniques that can be used by any parent to reduce stress and increase their enjoyment of the wonderful gift that has been given to them –their children, the reward of life.

First, spend some time identifying all the things that make you feel stressed.

Think of this activity as an investment in your health and happiness. Really listen to your body during this exercise and respond objectively to the questions that are inescapably provoked. Ask yourself the following questions: When do I feel nervous? When is my breathing shallow? When are my shoulders tensed? When am I likely to snap at the children or lose my patience? You may want to document or keep a journal of your responses in order to notice changeable and sustainable patterns.

In my practice, I coach clients on how to identify both external stressors like the demands of work and relationships, and internal stressors such as cognitive distortions, pain, and infections. Together, we use Reality Thinking strategies and a holistic-oriented program called: "**Evolution of Me**" to bring balance to their lives, identify healing opportunities and eliminate stressors that do not support the body to build health and happiness.

Personally, I try to live my life as stress free as possible, which is not always easy with the growth and expansion of Evolution of Me, speaking engagements, new projects, and consulting work. To counter stress, I eat a nutrient dense diet, read, meditate, and get adequate rest, and regular exercise. Additionally, I incorporate the following four principles in my regimen to keep me grounded:

1. **A Clear Sense of Purpose**. As a way of eliminating stress, I clarify what is most important, by focusing on one or two key objects and delegating the less important objects.
2. **Connecting to Nature**. Walking in the park, breathing in fresh air, and feeling the warmth of the sun on my skin energizes me and provide me with a valuable sense of inner peace.
3. **Relinquish Control**. I do so by surrounding myself with a team of talented individuals, colleagues, and friends with whom I share challenges and burdens as well as joys and successes.

Collaboration enables me to create a sense of community and shared responsibility.
4. **Laugh**. The act of laughter instantly relieves stress. Finding humor in my life and not taking myself too seriously has always been in my stress reduction arsenal. I have also found humor to be a great tool for breaking the ice and putting those around me at ease in otherwise stressful situations.

Second, re-engineer your routine

A study by Epstein suggests that *planning* is the most effective way to manage stress (Epstein, 2011) because it can prevent stress from occurring. For instance, for my morning to be calm and peaceful, I've learned to select my clothes for the following day at night, and I wake up a full 60 minutes earlier than necessary in order to complete meditation and exercise for that day.

Additionally, to avoid the routine stress of running late, I plan to arrive where I need to be 10 minutes early. Avoiding this stress not only makes my life feel easier (and therefore happier) but it leaves me with more energy to accomplish the things I need to complete on my task list.

Parents should carefully examine their daily routine. Get up at a certain time and review your priorities. Review them keeping in mind how everything can or will be affected by your interests. Some parents feel they do not have the luxury of time to make any effort. Remember, the first step of becoming aware of your actions and choices is the first step in making a difference in how you approach your daily lifestyle. Instituting reflective morning rituals can increase productivity, success, and health. It might even enable you to generate more income.

Third, proactively build your coping capacity

Let's face it: we cannot eliminate stress completely from our schedules. We plan to gain more control over our day, but if nothing else, parenting is an exercise in not being in control. So we need to build up our stress-busting muscles. Stress management is really a set of skills that we need to learn and practice for ourselves (and with our children). Research shows that the more hours we put into training ourselves to deal with stress—through yoga or relaxation techniques, for example—the happier and more stress-free our lives can be (Carter, 2011).

In addition to lifestyle changes that reduce stress, you need some strategies for dealing with the stressful events of parenting. Because some life events may be beyond your personal control, you will inevitably experience stressful periods. And you will find that some recurring experiences tend to be threatening whenever they occur. For example, the act of dealing with school issues, racism, finances or a strong-willed child.

Below is a list of stress management strategies or stress buffers (busters) to help you get started. Those that are relevant to your situation may be researched and used for dealing with the especially stressful parts of parenting:

Stress busters

- Meditation
- Prayer
- Exercise (see appendix 3)
- Aroma therapy
- Music
- Massage
- Reading
- Deep breathing
- Take a bath
- Take a walk
- Sleep
- Dance
- Relaxation
- Eat healthy
- Set boundaries
- Laugh
- Collaborate and cooperate

Forth, complete established priorities by managing yourself in time

It is tempting to react rather than respond all day long. For example, reacting to text messages, phone calls and emails or just being on auto pilot. At times, the things that seem most urgent are done at the expense of vital tasks on your priority list. Living this way tend to cost us what's most important – our health and happiness. My commitment, therefore, is to remain ever conscious of being culturally grounded while negotiating the main priorities in my daily routine:

- Maintain my own health and happiness
- Coach amazing human beings who are enthusiastic about becoming healthy and happy
- Help to heal our community one family at a time

When I skip exercise or short change myself on sleep, I become out of balance which put my immune system at risk. My energy becomes drained and I am not as productive as when I am in sync with my commitments and the universe. When I follow my priorities as planned, I am healthy and happy with myself. If I fail to maintain my health (the first priority), for example, this puts my other two priorities at risk. So I always remind myself: It takes less time to meditate in the morning than it does to recover from depression or the flu, when I get run down.

This puts into perspective the concept of time. Time is the most valuable resource parents have, yet they often squander it by harboring the following erroneous beliefs:

- It is okay to procrastinate
- I can sweat the small stuff
- Tasks will be done faster/better if I do them by myself
- I do not have the time

Keep in mind that the concept of time management is a misnomer. Parents' challenge is not to manage time, but to manage themselves in time. It is true that "everything requires time. It is the only true universal condition. All work takes place in time and uses up time. Yet most [parents] take for granted this unique, irreplaceable, and necessary resource. Nothing else, perhaps, distinguishes effective [parents] as much as the tender loving care of managing the self in time" (Drucker, 2015). Maybe the cardinal breakthrough in stress management is the awareness and practice of managing self in time. We do so by:

- Not procrastinating or putting things off; getting tasks over with which brings great satisfaction
- Avoiding needless worries that clog up your life – don't sweat the small stuff. Repeat and practice the serenity prayer
- Delegating tasks to significant others; experiencing the joy of age-appropriately training children to be assistants
- Recognizing that we all have the same amount of time to accomplish our priorities. When we do not have time to execute our priorities, it is usually a problem of (1) over commitment (having too many things on you plate) or (2) "wasting" too much time. In reality, "we cannot waste time, we can only waste ourselves" (Adams, 2003).

Because of the race-related challenges that further complicate rearing African-American children, parents are well advised to develop adaptive behaviors for functioning more effectively in society. Following is an Adinkera pictogram of the crocodile (denkyem) which symbolizes adaptability. It is a memorial for African-American parents who need to accommodate, not assimilate into the dominant culture. Adinkera are age-old visual symbols, originally created by the Akan people of Ghana that represent concepts of aphorism. They are the values of the Akan people that have stood the test of time over the centuries. The crocodile lives in the water, yet breathes the air, demonstrating an ability to adapt to circumstances.

DENKYEM

Adaptive behavior is a type of behavior that is used to adjust to another type of behavior or situation. This is characterized by skills that allow parents and children to change a non-constructive or destructive behavior to one that is more constructive. Adaptive skills are conceptual, social and practical skill-sets that are learned and used in daily life such as:

1. Self-Care – dressing, grooming, food handling and feeding one's self well (See The NEW START program in part one of this section)
2. Communication Skills – understanding and using verbal and nonverbal language (See chapter 8 on Parent/Child Communication) and
3. Self-Direction – safety, problem solving, exercising choice, initiating, planning and implementing activities; making reasonable decisions in the face of wide choices

In addition to these and other universal adaptive skills, African-American parents need to develop strategies for dealing with especially stressful events generated by racism. It has been established in the literature as well as in the media that racism and acts of violence due to racism are somewhat commonplace in America. Given this reality, African-American parents must accept the probability that their children will experience these inequalities as their contact with other racial groups increase. They must also prepare their children as best they can to respond, not react to racist experiences. The recommended preparation involves racial socialization, a major adoptive tool (Jones, 2010).

Racial socialization is generally defined as specific verbal and non-verbal messages transmitted to younger generations to develop values, attitudes, behaviors, and beliefs about the meaning and significance of **race** and **racial** stratification, intergroup and intragroup interactions, and personal and group identity. The object of racial socialization is to provide African-American children with a positive racial identity and a strong set of coping skills and habits necessary for participating within his or her social environment. In other words, racial socialization refers to parents' practices that teach children about their racial history or heritage and sometimes is referred to as pride development. The goal is to help children insulate themselves from and cope with the realities of racial discrimination.

Within the socialization literature, it has been determined that racially socializing one's children has positive effects for those children; but there is some ambiguity regarding the way it is best done. This disconnect between the clear need to racially socialize African-American children, and the somewhat vague understanding of how to accomplish this goal, may cause parents to feel helpless. Whaley and McQueen in their research on rites of passage administered by Family Renaissance, Inc., Brooklyn New York demonstrated through evidence-based outcomes that the disconnect referred to in the literature could be rectified with an Afrocentric curriculum (Whaley & McQueen, 2003). Research has found that racial-ethnic socialization buffers against negative experiences and promotes the well-being of Black youth (Benet, 2005 as cited in Whaley & McQueen, 2003).

Dr. Arthur Whaley's work also offers a conceptual framework or template for how racial socialization may be practiced. He developed the cognitive-cultural model of identity to explicate the process by which racial-ethnic socialization impacts racial-ethnic identity and subsequent social and behavioral outcomes among African-American adolescents. In this model, racial-ethnic identity in African-Americans is defined as cognitive schemata consisting of beliefs, attitudes, values, and behaviors that reflect a positive association with people of African descent (Whaley, 2003). That is, the individual's identity is composed of cognitive schemata representing the individual self, cultural self and social roles. When African-American youth do not have an adequate balance between these components of the self, they are likely to engage in risky behaviors and maladaptive functioning.

Adaptive behavior, then, must reflect an individual's social and practical competence in daily skills to meet the demands of everyday living. For the African-American child, competence must include knowledge of the individual, cultural and spiritual selves. Integration of these components of the self insulates them against low self-esteem. Indeed, behavior patterns change throughout a person's development and across life settings and social constructs such as changes in personal values, and the expectations of others. It is important to assess adaptive behavior, therefore, in order to determine how well an individual functions in daily life vocationally, socially, educationally, etc. Adaptive behavior includes age-appropriate behaviors necessary for people to live independently and to function safely, appropriately and stress-free in their environment.

To this end, here are seven (7) tips for helping parents of African-American descent to constantly adjust to naturally changing environments:

1. Recognize that you are not alone
2. Make your health a priority
3. Don't feel guilty or ashamed
4. Ask for help when required
5. Get needed child care
6. Request counseling, psychotherapy or life coaching as needed
7. Take only advice you value

My life coach teacher says it best: "Stress is the garbage of modern life." We don't need it, and life becomes unlivable when it builds up." After reading this section, plan to discard some stressful situations—get them out of your life! Apply relevant strategies outlined in this chapter to do what you can to avoid or eliminate all stressors. Your children will thank you for it.

References

Adams, George Matthews (2003). Stop Wasting Time. Retrieved from http://sidsavara.com/personal-development-stop-wasting-time-online-improve- concentration-online

Carter, Christine, PhD (2011). Is Stress Free Parenting Possible? Retrieved from http://greatergood.berkeley.berkeley.edu/raisinghappiness/post/managingstress Being a Parent Is the Most Important Job in the World. Retrieved form http://www.huffingtonpost.com/lorna-byrne/parenting-most-important-job-in-the-world_b_2034906.html, 2015.

Drucker, Peter F (2015). Time Management. Retrieved from http://sidsavara.com/personal-productivity/time-management-lies

Epstein, Robert Dr. (2014). How to Help People Manage Stress. Retrieved from <http://mystressmanagementskills.com/managers January 2015>

Kirby Deater-Deckard et al (2013). Parenting Stress. Retrieved from http://www.oxfordbibliographies.com/view/document/obo-9780199828340/obo-9780199828340-0142.xml?rskey=Pyed8a&result=1&q=parenting+stress#firstMatch, on 2015.

Thompson, Remy, Jones (2010). The effect of racial socialization on parental stress in a sample of African American parents. Retrieved form http://scholarscompass.vcu.edu/etd/2101/, 2015.

Whaley, A L (2004). *An Afrocentric Program as Primary Prevention for African-American Youth: Qualitative and Quantitative Exploratory Data. Journal of Primary Prevention*, 2004-Springer.

McQueen John P & Whaley, AL (2004).Ibid.

Co-Parenting for the Best Child Outcomes (Part I)

Author

Naila Smith, MA Fordham University

Norissa Williams, MSW, PhD Medgar Evers College at CUNY

"As parents, we guide by our unspoken example. It is only when we're talking to them that our kids aren't listening."

-Robert Brault

If you are like me[5] you may have cringed the first time you had to let your child spend a lengthy amount of time in the intimate space shared by your ex-spouse and their new partner. In fact, you might have even demonized this individual and been distasteful of them before knowing a thing about them. You might feel challenged, thinking, "He/she has a mother/father. He/she doesn't need another." You might even feel territorial about your child/children in whom you have invested so much blood, sweat and tears. In contrast, when you are the one who has a new partner, you may not know to what extent you should allow this new person to partner with you in the raising of your child, with hopes of still allowing space for their other biological or adoptive parent to be in the child's life in a meaningful way. If you *are* that new partner,

---

5   First-person anecdotal accounts are shared by second author.

Happy New Year

the same challenges and role confusion often applies. These emotional responses are normal. The exact nature of your feelings, however, will vary based on your current life circumstances and the nature of the break up that freed each partner to eventually pursue another partner. Nevertheless, despite those feelings there is one constant - a developing a child/children whose well-being should be the primary concern of all parties involved. In the remainder of this chapter we discuss the nature of shared parenting or co-parenting after separation or divorce and research-based best practices for co-parenting.

In the research literature the term "co-parenting" refers to two or more adults who share responsibility for rearing at least one child and must collaborate to meet their childrearing obligations (Feinberg, 2003; McHale & Lindahl, 2011; Teubert & Pinquart, 2010). The term "co-parents" can apply to both traditional (e.g. biological, cohabiting and married parents) and non-traditional families (e.g. gay-lesbian parents or fictive kin) and is often used to replace the term "step-parent" in the literature on separated or divorced partners. In this chapter, we specifically focus on co-parenting in blended families where a spousal or cohabitating relationship has been dissolved or is in the process of dissolution and a new family is being formed through remarriage or cohabitation (Gonzales, 2009).

Conceptual models of co-parenting suggest that there are multiple dimensions of co-parenting. Teubert & Pinquart (2010) proposed a synthesized model of co-parenting which identifies four dimensions: agreement, cooperation, conflict, and triangulation. Agreement is the extent to which each parents' thoughts and beliefs about child-related topics and issues, such as, child behavioral expectations or emotional needs, are similar (Feinberg, 2003). Cooperation is the exchange of information, joint decision-making and creation of a climate of mutual support, respect and loyalty as experienced by the child. It includes division of childrearing tasks and responsibilities such as after-school care, medical care and so on (Feinberg, 2003; Teubert & Pinquart, 2010). In contrast, conflict entails overt fights or arguments between parents about childrearing issues while triangulation is characterized by the involvement of the child in parental conflicts and the formation of a coalition between a child and one parent (Teubert & Pinquart, 2010). These dimensions of co-parenting are influenced by parent (e.g.

personality), family (e.g. household income), and child (e.g. disabilities) factors and have interactive and cumulative effects on child outcomes (Feinberg, 2003; Teubert & Pinquart, 2010).

Research findings indicate that these dimensions of co-parenting influence child outcomes in important ways (Teubert & Pinquart, 2010). Specifically, children whose parents show higher levels of cooperation and agreement in their co-parenting relationship tend to demonstrate lower levels of internalizing (e.g. depression or anxiety) and externalizing (e.g. aggression or hyperactivity) behavior problems, and higher levels of social functioning. Additionally, children whose parents showed higher levels of cooperation show higher levels of attachment to their parents. Conversely, children whose parents show higher levels of conflict and triangulation in their co-parenting relationship tend to show higher levels of internalizing and externalizing behavior problems and lower levels of attachment with parents. Children whose parents had higher levels of conflict also show poorer social functioning. Consequently, the findings from this growing body of work suggest that co-parenting practices that maximize agreement and cooperation and minimize conflict and triangulation among co-parents will likely produce the most adaptive child outcomes (Teubert & Pinquart, 2010). The following section briefly summarizes co-parenting issues encountered by blended families and some strategies suggested by research that co-parents can use to strengthen co-parenting and increase the likelihood of best child outcomes.

Co-parents should engage in ongoing, open dialogue as they negotiate and agree on expectations regarding new roles and responsibilities within blended families. The introduction of new adults into the co-parenting dynamic is one major way that roles and responsibilities must be negotiated in blended families. Members of the blended family should recognize that the joining of two families is a slow process that requires time to build close, trusting relationships (Adler-Baeder & Higginbotham, 2004). This process calls for flexibility and respect among family members, acknowledgement and ongoing reinforcement of the fact that the new co-parent is not a replacement for the non-residential, biological parent, and in-depth discussion of and clarification about the new co-parent's role and new rules of engagement concerning household functioning (Adler-Baeder & Higginbotham, 2004; Dupuis,

2007). New co-parents should take on parenting responsibilities gradually. They should first focusing on establishing a warm, trusting relationship with their non-biological child or children and take a supporting role when their spouse handles matters of discipline. Over time as relationships become stronger, the new co-parent can become more actively involved in the disciplining of children (Dupuis, 2007).

Agreement on roles and responsibilities is a prelude for separated or divorced parents to work cooperatively in order to make joint-decisions and manage day-to-day childrearing tasks, as well as, more long-term child-focused responsibilities. In order to ensure that they form a positive alliance, co-parents need to (1) create a plan for the sharing child-rearing responsibility; (2) engage in constructive communication about their children; (3) demonstrate respect for the other parent (Whiteside, 1998). A plan for sharing child-rearing responsibility typically includes consideration of how the child's time will be spent between the two households. This parenting time plan should be developmentally appropriate and change as children grow from childhood to late adolescence. For example, overnight visits with the non-residential parent are generally not recommended during the first few months of life infants need to have predictable and stable care and routines, however, as the child grows around 4-8 months, 1-2 overnight visits per month can be introduced and then increased over time (Hartson, 2010). Constructive communication among parents is critical for exchange of information and problem-solving. For example, when children are very young, parents need to discuss how to synchronize their children's routines (e.g. bedtime) across households to minimize the disruptive nature of different household schedules and practices (Whiteside, 1998). Finally, parents should demonstrate respect for the other parent in order to maintain a climate of harmony in the co-parent dyad. For example, calling the ex-partner disrespectful names or allowing the child to call the ex-partner disrespectful names would create an atmosphere of antagonism or distrust which would undermine the co-parenting dynamic and likely lead to conflict and triangulation.

Reducing conflict in the co-parenting relationship is critical to ensuring adaptive child outcomes. Disagreements are an unavoidable aspect of parenting and, not surprisingly, also characterize co-parenting dynamics. The frequency of conflict, however, is less important than the content of the conflict and the extent to which parents can arrive at a satisfactory resolution (Whiteside, 1998). It almost goes without saying that parents should minimize their child's exposure to hostile verbal arguments. However, the underlying tensions of highly conflictual parenting relationships will still have negative effects on child outcomes even if children are not directly exposed to arguments (Teubert & Pinquart, 2010; Whiteside, 1998). Parents whose relationships are highly conflictual with limited occasions of resolution should consider meeting with a therapist or mediator who can help by establishing safe and structured environments for parenting discussions and by teaching constructive conflict resolution techniques such as win/win negotiation strategies and re-framing conflictual issues from the child's perspective (Whiteside, 1998). Conflictual co-parenting can lead to triangulation of the child through the formation of parent-child coalitions. To prevent triangulation from happening, parents should avoid speaking negatively about their ex-partner to their child, forcing the child to choose sides or enlisting the child's help in berating the other parent during an argument (Feinberg, 2003).

For purposes of application in the Black family, it might be useful to consider these statistics: Black female-head of households in America were just 18 percent of households in 1950, as opposed to 68 percent in 2015 (Williams, 2014). In fact, from 1890-1940, the Black marriage rate was slightly higher than that of Whites. Even during slavery, when marriage was forbidden for Blacks, most Black children lived in biological two-parent families. In New York City in 1925, 85 percent of Black households were two-parent households. A study of 1880 family structure in Philadelphia shows that three quarters of Black families were two-parent households (Williams, 2014).

The increase in Black female–headed households is due to several factors, including lack of Black male income, the poverty rate among Blacks is 36 percent, most of which is found in female-headed households. Along with the decline of the Black family is anti-social behavior, manifested by high crime rates (Williams, 2014). Because of the exceedingly high rate of father-absent children that continues to emerge in Black households, it behooves Black parents to embrace and apply the co-parenting strategies embodied in this chapter for cultivating loving relationships with their children. At the same time, they will be insulating themselves and their children from falling victims to negative stereotypes as well as becoming sadistic statistics.

In conclusion, when intimate partnerships dissolve, working together to ensure the best outcomes for the children produced during the partnership should remain the central focus of all adults involved. Co-parenting is a multidimensional concept that is associated with children's social and emotional development in important ways. It is most effective when parents' communicate constructively, engage in ongoing dialogue and negotiation of roles and responsibilities, use effective conflict resolution strategies and ensure children do not become triangulated in parental conflict.

References

Adler-Baeder, F., & Higginbotham, B. (2004). Implications of remarriage and stepfamily formation for marriage education. *Family Relations*, *53*(5), 448–458.

Dupuis, S. B. (2007). Examining remarriage: A look at issues affecting remarried couples and the implications towards therapeutic techniques. *Journal of Divorce & Remarriage*, *48*(1/2), 91–104.

Feinberg, M. E. (2003). The internal structure and ecological context of co-parenting: A framework for research and intervention. *Parenting: Science & Practice*, *3*(2), 95.

Gonzales, J. (2009). Pre-family counseling: Working with blended families. *Journal of Divorce & Remarriage*, *50*(2), 148–157. doi:10.1080/10502550802365862

Hartson, J. N. (2010). Children with two homes: Creating developmentally appropriate parenting plans for children ages zero to two. *American Journal of Family Law*, *23*(4), 191–199.

McHale, J. P., & Lindahl, K. M. (2011). *Co-parenting: A conceptual and clinical examination of family systems*. (J. P. McHale & K. M. Lindahl, Eds.). Washington, DC, US: American Psychological Association.

Teubert, D., & Pinquart, M. (2010). The association between co-parenting and child adjustment: A meta-analysis. *Parenting: Science & Practice*, *10*(4), 286–307. doi:10.1080/15295192.2010.492040

Whiteside, M. F. (1998). The parental alliance following divorce: An overview. *Journal of Marital and Family Therapy*, *24*(1), 3–24. doi:10.1111/j.1752-0606.1998.tb01060.x

The Fatherhood Factor: Impact of a Father's Absence (Part II)

Author

O'Neil Richards, LCSW

President, OSR Consultants LLC

Therapist, Center for Psychotherapy

> "There is a crisis in America. According to the US Census Bureau, 24 million children in America - one out of three – live without their biological dad in their lives. Consequently, there is a father factor in nearly all of the societal [problems] facing us. We must realize there is a father absence crisis and begin to raise more involved, responsible, and committed fathers."
>
> **--Ryan Sanders**

Ninety-eight percent of my clients, children of African Descent, wrestle with unresolved childhood issues with their fathers or father figures. This condition is referred to as the father-absent wound, which continue to haunt them in their adult life. The impact (positive or negative) of father's absence in our homes, neighborhood, and communities cannot be overemphasized. This is especially so when some of the essential roles of a father such as nurturer, protector, and provider are taken into consideration.

In addition, fathers are expected to help facilitate the development of children's self-identity, boost their self-esteem and enable them to make healthy adjustments to the outer world. While many desire the ideals inherent in father's status and role designations as specified above, the reality is that many families of African descent are dealing with the stark reality of the literal physical absence of the father/father figure and the attendant emotional and spiritual deficits that accompany this condition. In this chapter, I will discuss a few salient points pertaining to fathers and father absence and share a case example to highlight the negative impact of a father's absence and to validate the importance of psychotherapy as a mechanism for psychosocial, emotional and spiritual healing.

What is a father?

According to Merriam-Webster Dictionary (online), a father is "a man who has begotten a child." Dictionary.com defines father as a male "parent"; "a father-in-law, stepfather, or adoptive father." These are denotative definitions related to the title.

My questions to you are: How do you define father? What makes you or him a good enough daddy? What are some of the characteristics of a good enough father? Who modeled this role (father) to you and how old were you (child, adolescent, young adult...all your life) when this modeling took place?

Roles of a father Traditional and contemporary:

Many of us grew up with the idea that fathers are supposed to provide financially, fix things around the house, be strong and protect the family. According to Dr. Myles Munroe, tradition has it that, the men bring home the bacon and the women prepare it. Many of us remember this being true in the household(s) we grew up in. On the contrary, today's households look a lot different from what we grew up in. While in many cases it is true that the men are bringing home the bacon, in today's world, the women are bringing home the pig. Some families are choosing to have the dad/father stay home and take care of the children while the mother works. Some have women/mothers who generate more income than their male partners. For some families, financial demands force both parents to work; thus, leaving less time for them to interact with each other and with their children. Many families struggle with the reality of the new/non-traditional family structure and unfortunately, many fathers have chosen to physically and/or mentally "check-out" from the home.

Reasons why fathers disengage:

There are thousands of reasons associated with why fathers disengage, leave or separate from their families of procreation. Research, however, indicates that they disengage due to absent-mindness, physical separation, imprisonment, divorce, unemployment, single mothers by choice, illness, and death. However, I am narrowing my list to what I believe to be the significant five:

I. First, for some fathers, they are unequipped (lack the knowledge-base and skill sets) to deal with the above-mentioned list of traditional roles. This level of unpreparedness is often enough for them to check-out and leave their families of procreation physically and/or mentally barren. Others justify their actions with the reasoning that they are not equipped with the resources necessary fulfilling the contemporary role of a father. Those fathers' identities that are defined by their role as provider, "the bread winner," they have a hard time adjusting to the contemporary roles of fathers. Thus, many are seeking a place, a home, where they can comfortably play their traditional roles in lieu of their more contemporized family of procreation.

II. Second, some fathers separate from their families of procreation because they no longer get along with of have become emotionally distant from the mothers of their children. In many cases doing, they leave, and often divorce the children along with the mother. Still others are growing up and have chosen to remain at the developmental stage of "adolescence," thus never taking on "adult responsibilities."

III. Third, some fathers have disengaged because they are disillusioned with the issues/challenges of being the parent of a needy/special-needs child and have consigned the responsibilities of raising such children to their mothers.

IV. Fourth, others remain at home physically but are mentally and emotionally absent.
V. Fifth, still others; disengage because the act or role of being a father has opened/triggered old and unresolved wounds/trauma with their own fathers. As a result, instead of taking appropriate actions to heal that generational father-absent wound, they secretly choose, albeit unconsciously, to separate from their children. Thus, they continue the cycle of physical, emotional and spiritual father absent. These fathers are those who suffer deep, complicated and life altering wounds. Some wounds/impact is visible and others are invisible or imperceptible.

The impact of the father's absence in communities of African Descent:

Obviously, defining the role of a father in today's society with yesterday's designations can be a recipe for disaster. The situation is exacerbated by the fact that many fathers are clueless as to what their roles are and the impact of their absence on children. Some admit that they never knew the effect father absence had on the children they left behind because of their preoccupation with fulfilling their own needs. Others acknowledge that they have learned to numb/distract themselves from thinking or feeling the impact. The findings of an ACE (Adverse Childhood Experiences) study, "Oklahoma KIDS COUNT," illustrate this point: "When separation occurs, children may lose out on the protection and nurturance...and can experience the deprivation of parental attention. In many cases, fear of loss and disaster shape the choices of these children as they grow, leading to...and [indulging] in greater use of drugs and alcohol."

Many children report seeing father absence as a reflection of something they have done wrong. As a result, this undesirable perception is internalized. They are therefore habituated into feeling guilty (remorse for having done something wrong) and/or being ashamed (remorse for being wrong). Consequently, fatherless children may display symptoms such as (a) being withdrawn (not wanting to cause waves) (b) avoiding eye contact and conflict (avoid advocating for or asserting themselves) (c) low self-esteem and poor self/body image (d) cutting/self-mutilation (e) being combative/argumentative (f) engaging in fights and fits of rage (g) participating in promiscuous behaviors which may lead to unplanned/teenage pregnancy (h) being easily influenced by criminal activity (gang, prostitution, drug dealing, etc.) and (i) increased risk for mental illness, substance abuse.

Specifically, anecdotal observation and published research reveal that:

Father-absent girls may not feel sure about their femininity. They may have unrealistic expectations about what men are like, may doubt their sexual attractiveness and may seek father substitutes in romantic relationships. Additionally, they may stay in abusive and unrewarding relationships longer than is in their best interest (McQueen, 2003).

Father-absent boys may have an undeveloped sense of what it means to be a man. They may have insufficient self-discipline, and may display confusion about career direction. They may be driven obsessively to seek validation through recognition, money and power. They may also have faulty preparation for male/female relationships (McQueen, 2003).

Many of the men/fathers who have been "abandoned' as children are unable to connect deeply with significant others, including their own children because they have never had such experiences modeled to them. The absence of their own fathers robbed them of the opportunity – the gift, if you will - of learning how to communicate and interact meaningfully with their spouse or child's mother, significant others, and their children. In short, they do not know how to be fathers, and how to authentically relate to the world around them. Many do not have a blue print, guide or model of what they are supposed to do.

How do you measure a man? Is it strength of his fist, his money, status, or the size and agility of his penis? These are value-added characteristics. However, according to Na'im Akbar, manhood means self-definition. Yes, men respect themselves and their families, men control their environment, men defend their resources, and men build institutions (Akbar, 2005). Indeed, healthy men are creative, resourceful and whole. Whole men therefore attract whole women and produce wholesome children. On the other hand, father absent females, tend to make secrete or unconscious choices in selecting emotionally unhealthy men who have not healed their father-absent wound.

Father absent women are predisposed to go from one relationship to the next unaware that they are trying in vain to find love and acceptance from dad in the men they are dating. Accordingly, some stay in unhealthy relationships where they are subjected to physical, emotional, psychological and even sexual abuse. Some sisters have turned their disappointment with absentee fathers into anger and rage. They, therefore, take on the more dominant role in relationships by putting down or castrating men whenever the opportunity presents itself. These females seek out men who are passive, indecisive, agreeable, and/or emotionally deprived. It is important for father-absent women to keep in mind that "they cannot separate from what they need and never had until find it or its equivalent" (McQueen, 2002). The quality of emotional work required for healing the father absent wound or "the hole in the soul in the shape of fathers" may be accomplished in a therapeutic environment.

Addressing the impact of a father's absence:

Indeed, father absence is one of the greatest social problems in America. However, children with absentee fathers can be healthy and well-adjusted when they receive psychotherapeutic help and/or when they obtain support from other male adults who are positive male role models. Needless to say, the emphasis on fatherhood is not intended as a slight against single mothers or the institution of motherhood. Instead, it seeks to highlight the unique role of fathers, their contribution to the healthy development of children, as well as, the negative impact of a father's absence.

Amazingly, children and people in general are resilient – they have the ability to bounce back from setbacks. This is epitomized in the words of the adage: "a set- back is really a set-up for a comeback." Healing the father-absent wound, therefore, could be facilitated through self-help or psychotherapy by utilizing the following process:

- First, is the recognition that you or someone you are in a relationship with is suffering from the father-absent wound.
- Second, is the acknowledgment that you or your loved one has the ability to heal the 'hole in your soul' emanating from father's absence.

- Third, is the examination phase of treatment. Socrates posits that "The unexamined life is not worth living." The wounded, therefore, should take some time to heal themselves from all the lies they have told themselves and all the lies that have been told to them." In this middle phase of treatment, wounded souls contemplate, forgive and explore how father's absence has impacted their lives; the status of their current and past relationship(s) with significant others, their children, at work (supervisors/co-workers), with friends, religious leaders (Pastors, etc.), mentors, etc. You may also want to keep a journal as a way of recognizing patterns.
- Finally, if this work seems too overwhelming or challenging for you to tackle by yourself, you may want to find a good therapist and begin the journey of addressing the physical, emotional and spiritual impact of father's absence in your life. This might be in individual, couple, family or group therapy.

The prevalence of absent fathers in the Black neighborhoods suggests that this social problem is affecting thousands of families in your circles. And it may have profound emotional, psychological, spiritual, developmental, educational and legal consequences. Abandoned children are advised to turn to psychotherapy. It is a healthy way of resolving psycho-spiritual issues that affect not only affected individuals, but also families, communities, and society in general. Following is a case example of a client system that embraced and benefited from psychotherapy to address issues related to father absence.

A Case Example

The couple Ben and Jen (pseudonyms) came to the center for Psychotherapy because they were having a lot of conflicts in their relationship and it was progressively getting worse. The couple is African American, in their early 30s, and they have 2 children together (12 y/o boy and 10 y/o girl). The husband, Ben, met his father briefly for the first time when he was 15 years old. The connection with his father was short lived because he (Ben's father) was killed violently during a robbery. Ben moved around within his maternal extended family system for a while before living steadily with his aunt. Periodically he would stay with his mother for weekends and holidays. While growing up, he witnessed his mother and aunts being physically abused by the men in their lives. Ben has his GED but never attended college. He works for a well-known company but he does not like his job because it is very stressful. He reports that he stays with this company because it pays well and he cannot afford to quit at this time. He shared also that his wife, Jen, insists that he remains in his current job because of the benefits he derives from it.

The wife, Jen, grew up with both parents and 3 other siblings. However, she reported that her father was always busy working for the community and did not have time for her or her siblings. She recalled that he was cold and dismissive of her thoughts and feelings. She reported that her mother was always submissive to her father and that both her and her siblings felt that her mother should have been more assertive with their father. According to Jen, her mother was very pretty, younger than her father, and more educated. However, he did not allow her to work. Jen recently received her Bachelor's degree but works part-time at a clothing store which pays minimum wage. According to Jen, the job is physically demanding with no benefits. She does not have any plans to seek another job at this time because Ben feels that her current job hours allow her the opportunity to pick-up their children from school.

During therapeutic sessions, it was revealed that Jen was sexually abused by a close family member when she was between the ages of 9 and 17 years. Even though her family knew her situation, no one did anything about it. When she told her father he tried to mediate the circumstances with her and the individual, but with little or no success. Jen's chief complaint in her current marital relationship was that her husband is cold, emotionally absent, dismissive and controlling. Ben's chief complaint: my wife is smothering, needy, and selfish.

Due to deficits in relational knowledge and skills, the couple was unable, by themselves, to deconstruct the negative impact of father absence on their marriage. They were unable to see that they were acting out childhood desires and fantasies related to their poor or missing relationships with their fathers. In symbolic terms, Jen married her father, and Ben was unable to connect with Jen because he did not have a blueprint to follow that enabled him to connect with his wife. During our sessions, we explored their up-bringing (family of origin issues including what their current family of procreation looked like), expectations of the relationship (realistic and unrealistic), marital structure, gender roles (traditional and contemporary), money, goals, and parenting styles. The exploration of these issues helped the couple to address and repair their shared experiences of the impact father's absence.

Yes, "I felt [father's] absence," Jane said. "It was like waking up one day with no teeth in my mouth. I didn't need to run to the mirror to know they were gone." Father absence is truly pervasive in the African-American culture. Indeed, it is one of the greatest social problems the Black family faces today. To foster fully functioning adults, mental health professionals are poised to help father-absent children heal the father absent wound – healing body, mind and soul.

Below is a table displaying a popular cultural symbol of the Akan people of Ghana, West Africa with its African and accompanying English translation highlighting its literal, symbolic and proverbial meanings. The three visual images of SANKOFA are constant reminders of the need for children of African descent of to return and fetch their cultural heritage - the spiritual foundation which expresses a particular attitude or behavior related to a father's presence in the lives of his children (see Adinkera symbol in chapter five on Parenting Styles).

SANKOFA SYMBOLS

Adinkera Symbol	Literal Meaning	Symbolic Meaning	Proverbial Expression
	Return and get it.	You can always correct your mistakes	See wo were fin a wo Sankofa ayennkyi
	Learning from the past.	Wisdom of learning from past experiences to build the future	
	Go back to fetch it,	Better late than never	It is not a taboo to return to fetch something you forgot earlier on

References

ACE issue brief 5: Absent Parents *Findings of the Adverse Childhood Experience (ACE) Study* Oklahoma KIDS COUNT Factbook, 2006–2007 Issue Brief 5 of 5

Biel, L. & Peske, N. (2005).*Raising A Sensory Smart Child. The Definitive Handbook for Helping Your Child with Sensory Integration Issues.* New York: Penguin Group.

Carter, B. & McGoldrick, M. (Eds.). (2005). *The expanded family Life Cycle: individual, family, and social perspectives* (3rd ed.). Boston: Allyn & Bacon.

Curry, J. F., Wells, K. C., Brent, D. A., Clarke, G. A., Rohde, P., Albano, A. M., Reinecke, M. A., Benazon, N. And March, J. S. (2005).Treatment for adolescents with depression study (TADS). Cognitive behavioral therapy manual*: introduction, rationale, and adolescent sessions.* North Carolina: Duke University Medical Center.

Fraser, M. W. (Ed.). (2004). *Risk and resilience in childhood: an ecological perspective* (2nd ed.). Washington, DC: NASW Press.

Kazdin, A. E., & Weisz, J. R. (Eds.). (2003). *Evidence-based psychotherapies for children and adolescents.* New York: The Guilford Press.

McQueen, John P. (2003). *The Impact of a Father's Absence. Kuji Magazine. Brooklyn* (Research findings from Galati and Sing, 1987).

McQueen (2002). Father's Absence. McQueen & Associates. Brooklyn. New York

Munroe, M., (2001).*Understanding the Purpose and Power of Men: a book for men and the women who love them.* New Kensington, PA: Whitaker House.

Newman, B. M., & Newman, P. R. (2006).*Development through life: a psychological approach* (9thed.). Belmont, CA: Thomson Wadsworth.

Woititz, J. G., (1993). *The Intimacy Struggle: Revised and Expanded For All Adults.* Deerfield Beach, Fl: Health Communications, Inc.

Money Management Basics for Parents & Children of African Descent (Part I)

Author

Ronald Richardson, BA & Financial Consultant

Former Certified Financial Planner & Personal Financial Analyst with Primerica

"Financial literacy is just as important in life as the other basics."

--John W. Rogers, Jr

The sentiment expressed in John Rogers' quotation above is as true as the gospel itself. That's why this chapter seeks to help parents of African descent reverse the money-talk "freeze" in families highlighted in the statement by ING Direct as follows: "In some families talking about money can be more uncomfortable than talking about sex." (ING Direct; June 8, 2009).

In this section, therefore, I will discuss money management basics in a way that enables parents to educate their children on money matters. While I will not use the sophisticated and unfamiliar language of the financial industry to discuss the subject matter, I will share the industry's time-tested ideas and solutions for engaging parents and children in financial literacy. The goal is to help parents explore ways to successfully manage debt, learn how to create a budget and learn how to create a financial game plan.

With respect to raising children, they will understand the power of money by witnessing their parents' behavior and the family's financial culture long before they are developmentally ready for a conversation about money. From the cradle, children monitor how their parents manage finances, analyze the money-language expressed by their parents and often get their parents to satisfy their fleeting wants. In teachable moments, parents should have ongoing age-appropriate conversations regarding the cost of operating households, how to earn and not beg for money, and how to research the possibility of lowering costs. In effect, parents can teach money matters to children by monitoring their language about money and pointing out money lessons in non-pressured moments.

"In 2008, when asked about the negative consequences of debt, a higher percentage of African Americans reported being closer to bankruptcy, called by bill collectors or having their cars repossessed. In 2008, 81 percent of credit card-indebted African Americans, 58 percent of Hispanics and 54 percent of Whites had been called by bill collectors. In the same year, 37 percent of Hispanics, 34 percent of African Americans and 18 percent of Whites had a settlement agreement with a credit card company. Furthermore, in other areas like car repossession, African American and Hispanics are more likely to have their car repossessed" (The Color of Debt: Credit Card Debt by Race and Ethnicity).

Why is the aforementioned grim statistics the way they are? Do they reflect today's reality? Obviously, we can have several responses to the first question. As it relates to the second question, one thing is certain; parents of African descent, in large numbers, continue to play the financial game without fully understanding the rules and the consequences that may result from ignorance of the rules. As noted in Investopedia Staff, one such rule is the Rule of 72. Basically, this rule explains how long it takes money to double. This is the way it works: the number 72 is divided by the interest gained on your money. The result is the amount of time it takes your initial investment to double.

For example, if you have an initial investment of $10,000 and you are receiving 3 percent interest, it will take 24 years for it to double, (72/3 = 24). At 12 percent, it will take 6 years for your initial investment to double, (72/12 = 6). At 24 percent, it will take 3 years for your initial investment to double. We are all aware that there are no banks paying 24 percent interest on money saved. The banks and credit card companies operate by this rule. They therefore lend money to generate big profits based on this principle. For example, a $10,000 loan at 24 percent interest (the highest interest rate charged by most lenders), would double in three years. Obviously, if your debt is growing faster than your savings, your debt burden will be continually higher. Hence, the need to address this discrepancy is crucial if we are to make real progress in our financial matters.

There are several ways to manage debt successfully. Keep in mind that not all debt is necessarily "bad" debt. For example, a student loan may be a good debt because it's an investment in the student's education for future higher earning potential and upward mobility. In order for us to truly solve the debt/earnings ratio, we must first have to determine what debt we owe. This requires contacting our creditors, getting copies of our credit score and report from all three credit bureaus (Equifax, Experian, and Transunion), then listing our credit obligations in order of highest to lowest interest rates being paid. The purpose of this is for you to pay off your highest interest debt first which reduces the overall cost of your debt. This process also requires that we examine our attitude about spending and acquiring income. Finally, we need to come up with a game plan for minimizing or eliminating debt in order to begin building positive net worth.

Now that we have gathered all information on whom we owe and what is it we owe for, the next task is to create the cornerstone of our debt reduction program, a budget. Budgeting and financial planning for the family should involve all those who are part of the household and must also include your dreams, goals and resources. A successful budget plan requires the full participation and support of the entire family. When family members are on board, they will work to help find solutions rather than create obstacles to progress. One way to get everyone on board is by sharing your vision with family members. It is important that each family member understands why the goal is important to the family's wellbeing and what accomplishing this goal will enable the family to have and enjoy. Emphasize the payoff of putting in hard work and sacrifice.

For example, if you want to save for a vacation, then the family may have to sacrifice the amount of times they go out for dinner and other recreational pursuits in order to enjoy time together on the family vacation. This is called increasing the ability to delay gratification.

In your budget, I recommend that you sort your expenses into three categories: (1) **Your needs:** this includes shelter, food, water, clothing, warmth, family safety, healthcare and transportation. (2) **Your wants:** these are conveniences such as cable Television and cellular phones with data plans; and (3) **Luxury items**: these are such items as dream or indulgence vacations. Keep in mind that a need is something your family has to have, something they cannot do without. A good example is food. If they don't eat, they won't survive for too long. A want is something your family would like to have but could do without. It is not absolutely necessary, but would be a good thing to have. A good example is music. The family does not need music to survive, but they do need to eat. Once you have figured out your expenses, remember your needs come first.

Review each category and consider ways to reduce those expenses. There will be times when you will have more expenses than income. This is referred to as a *shortfall*. If you have a shortfall, after you have calculated your expenses, consider the following options: do not completely cut out any of your basic needs. This can have adverse effects on your overall financial game plan. For instance, do not sacrifice paying on your insurance to cover a shortfall. It would be best to look to save money by shopping around for bargains on food and clothing items. You can also increase your income by working overtime, taking on a part time job, considering a career change, or by selling something – anything that increases value. I would also recommend that you complete the attached budget sheets each month as a family activity, and as a way of measuring progress made. (See budget sheet in appendix 4).

Having family discussions is a great way to generate creative solutions rather than just focusing on problems. "When your children ask frank questions about your finances, try to view it as a teaching opportunity rather than a breach of privacy" (Torabi, Farnoosh, 2014). One way to give a practical lesson to children about money is to give them an allowance. The allowance should not be for basic jobs that the family does around the house. It should be given for jobs that are above and beyond the usual chores. The allowance could be divided in the following manner: one third is saved; one third is shared and one third is for spending. This way, children will learn the value of sacrificing for obtaining future financial goal. They will also learn the value of giving and sharing and the rewards for going above and beyond.

Once you have identified your debt owed, you have created a working budget, and have gotten all family members on board; it is now time to create a complete financial game plan. For your financial game plan to be successful, it must be written down. Writing crystallizes thought and thought motivate action. It should also consist of the seven P's as follows:

- **PRESENT TENSE** –present tense uses the verb's base form (write, work), or, for third-person singular subjects, the base form plus an -s ending (he writes, she works).
- The present tense indicates that an action is present, now, relative to the speaker or writer. Generally, it is used to describe actions that are factual or habitual -- things that occur in the present but that are not necessarily happening right now; something scheduled. For example, "In our game plan the family **achieves** $1000.00 emergency fund within the next three months."
- **POSITIVE** – a positive mental attitude is the act of responding positively to every situation in the family. It means to strongly believe that everything in the family is 'good'. It is believed that happiness and unhappiness are defined by our assumptions and it does not depend on what we are facing in reality. In short, we can say that, "our attitude decides our altitude." For example, "Our emergency fund of $1, 000 is established to help the family in case of unforeseen, precarious situations. It is a sacrifice, but it helps us delay gratification by scheduling the pain and pleasure of life in such a way as to enhance the pleasure by meeting and experiencing the pain first and getting it over with."
- **PERSONAL** – refers to one of the pronouns I, thou, he, she, it and their plurals; it pertains to or is characteristic of a person, a self-conscious being or an entity such as the family or a group; a brief and private statement in a family's game plan that are

embraced and owned by everyone. For example, "Many people do not know what to do or where to turn in a crisis. Our financial game plan consists of a $1000in case of any family emergency." An emergency is a sudden unforeseen situation or crisis (usually involving danger) that requires immediate action.

- **PURPOSEFUL** – means that which serves as or indicative of the existence of a purpose or goal; having meaning through having an aim; adding value to the family's functioning. For example, "Including a $1000 emergency funds in our family's game plan is a value-added benefit; it makes us feel secure."
- **PREDICTABLE** – implies *that which is foretold or declared in advance; a goal that* is measurable and is expected or anticipated. The roots of the word are fun to analyze: *pre* - means "before," *dict* means "to say," and *able* means, well, "able." Put them together, and you'll see that *predictable* means "able to be said before (it happens)" or, simply, something each family member knows before it happens. For example, *"Our* emergency fund has $1000 in three months."
- **PROACTIVE** – or pro-activity refers to the family rule, guiding principle, plan of action, process or stimulus that has an effect on events that occur subsequently. It is the act of controlling a situation by causing something to happen rather than waiting to react to it after it happens. For example, "Our need for security, love, belongingness, and understanding are all met in the act of preparing to, intervene in, or control any unexpected occurrence or situation. We are now initiating change rather than reacting to events by having our emergency fund of $1000 in place. This also serves as a teaching tool for helping children with planning ahead.
- **PRECISE** – signifies accuracy, exactness, and definiteness of purpose; sharply exact or accurate or delimited. For example, "Through a definite or exact statement the family decision is to establish a $1000 in our emergency fund that is available in three months." *In other words, our family's* game plan accomplishes what it says it will accomplish in the specified timeframe.

The structure of a financial game plan ought to be divided into two phases: (1) the accumulation phase and (2) the distribution phase. In the accumulation phase you are younger, you have young children, are working, probably have purchased a new home, have a high debt burden and low savings. The need for insurance (income replacement) is necessary in this phase of the family life cycle. In the distribution phase, your children are grown, your home is paid off, your debt burden is less, and you're retired. The need for cash is necessary in the distribution phase. The successful transition from the accumulation phase to the distribution phase depends on how well you manage your debt. The goal is to pay down your consumer debt, improve your credit score, also known as FICO score, and develop sufficient savings for retirement (a FIN number). When your financial game plan is done correctly you will be able to fill-in the blanks that follows, easily and confidently.

- I owe exactly $_____ in personal debt.
- I will be completely debt free by (date)_____.
- My FICO score (credit score) is _____.
- My FIN number (amount of money I need saved for retirement)_____.
- The value of the inheritance for children and grandchildren is _____.
- The location of my 'love box' (safe place where all important financial documents are kept for retrieval by my love ones in case I become ill or incapacitated _____.

What is a FICO score? "A FICO score is a credit score developed by FICO, a company that specializes in what's known as predictive analytics, which means they take information and analyze it to predict what is likely to happen. FICO scores range from 300 to 850. Your FICO score helps lenders determine what interest rate to give you, and many insurers use it to determine your premiums. How important is your FICO score? If you are buying a house, car, getting insurance, or even applying for a job, it can be critical. A low score can prevent you from renting the apartment you want or, worse yet, make you ineligible for certain jobs. Surprisingly, so much is riding on this number, but research show that very few parents of African descent understand how the FICO score is calculated, what the score represents, or what can be done to improve the score. Indeed, it is time to intelligently get into the financial game plan.

NKONSONKONSON

The Adinkra symbol of unity, responsibility, interdependence, brotherhood, and cooperation as depicted above symbolizes how sound financial game plans could best be orchestrated, developed, operated and maintained by families of African descent. The symbol evokes a storehouse of ancestral power. History is memory which potentially helps people to shape, fashion, and form their own identity. Cultural identity refers to the descriptive characteristics, qualities, and abilities that people use to define themselves. Without a sense of identity, the richest man, woman or child is poor. Void of cultural memory, the majority of people in the African Diaspora does not or cannot extend their memory beyond slavery and the civil rights movement. As a corrective, you are invited to study from our book list in glossary appendix seven in order to begin extending your memory into history for the purpose of capturing the cultural wealth that fuels strength and resiliency (see the meaning of Sankofa in chapter 14, p122).

Dr. John Henrik Clarke observed: "The task of Africans at home and abroad is to restore to their memory what slavery and colonization made them forget…in most of Africa, the job was so complete it was tantamount to a brain transplant." So what does Dr. Clarke's statement have to do with you, your children and your family's financial game plan? Everything! People of African descent who are consciously connected to their culture are able to unite, collaborate, cooperate, and reproduce the best of their ancestral kinship-bond, the financial plan which facilitated our fore parents' survival while taking the genius of their economic plan to the next level.

The construct, unity in spirit and action, involves the understanding that family and community involvement depends upon building strong relationships and interdependent activities. The symbolism and imagery is intended to help parents of African descent conceptualize and explore ways to successfully manage debt, learn how to create a budget and learn how to develop and sustain a financial game plan in the context of community. Our transformation as a people is inherent in the Kwanzaa principle of Ujima (collective work and responsibility). We only have, "to build and maintain our own stores, shops, and other business and to profit from them together." Ujima is the ultimate financial game plan for children in the African Diaspora.

References

1. Garcia, Jose: 2010; "The Color of Debt: Credit Card Debt by Race and Ethnicity@ www.demos.org/publication/color-debt.

2. "The Rule of 72" Investopedia Staff @ www.investopedia.org

3. Torabi, Farnoosh: "Mommy Are We Rich" Money Magazine, Nov 2014, page 33.

Money Management Basics for Parents of African Descent (Part II)

<u>Author</u>

Artis Harry, LMSW

Therapist: Lincoln Hospital & Center for Psychotherapy

"The habit of saving is itself an education. It encourages every virtue. It teaches self-denial. It cultivates the sense of order; it trains to forethought and so broadens the mind."

--Thornton T. Munger

If you were to think deeply about the world's best cricketers, basketball players, musicians, movie stars, and singers, you will discover that they have one basic thing in common: they practice, practice, practice! Practice is fundamental to their success. In other words, to excel or become the best in their respective fields, they all have spent countless hours practicing their skills. The reality is that skill mastery in any venture cannot be attained, unless one continuously and continually practices. Therefore, contained in this chapter, are tried and true tips, for helping parents develop money-management skills based on my personal experience.

My working definition for money management is the act or practice of managing or properly handling one's personal finances. I want you to make this personal, so I ask that you repeat after me: "Money management is the way I manage or handle whatever money I have." You may want to repeat this sentence again and again until it imprints your mind. Although the dollar amounts involved may be small, those of us who learn to control a small amount of money and practice their skill like a musician or the artists mentioned above, have a significant advantage over those parents with no financial training. So, please repeat after me: "It's not the dollar amounts that matter; it's the practicing i.e. forming a habit of saving or putting away part of the little money I have that will make a significant difference over time." Did you get it yet?

I habitually begin a task with the end in mind. Why is that you may ask? Well, based on this principle, "the end" becomes the long term goal and beyond. Parents who want to become successful money managers should always keep this principle in mind. As a parent, if you do not focus on the long term goal and beyond as it relates to money management, your practice will decrease and your money management skills will gradually be lost. In this regard, you will not attain your goals like your favourite cricketer, basketball player, musician, movie star, and singer. Why? This is because you have failed to practice.

Following are five additional techniques which I have used as part of my money-management basic strategies. These methods include finding out how much debt you owe, developing a monthly budget, paying down your credit card debt (if any), preparing your own food, and shopping with a grocery list, especially during sale events.

Finding out how much you owe:

As a parent, it's your responsibility to make sure that the needs of your family are met. For that to happen, it is very important that you learn, and practice the art of managing your money. It is a skill that will take time to develop, and it needs practice, much like the practice of your favorite athlete, sports figure, or singer does to stay on top of her or his game. Do you see the point? I hope you are paying close attention, because I don't want to lose you here. Stay with me on this point. To develop money management skills, you must plan and practice. Say it with me: "I will plan and practice money management skills." Excellent!

Here is an easy way to find out how much you owe. Collect each of your individual bills and find the balance due. It is good to keep track of this information going forward. You may do so by using a note book purchased from a 99 cents department store. For those parents who are able to use the computer, you may create a spreadsheet document to keep a record. Further, you should consider signing up for online access to each of your credit card and utility companies. This is to ensure that you can check your balance and payment information easily and frequently. What am I really saying here? I am indicating that organization is extremely essential if you want to keep up to date with your monthly bills. Now that you understand this principle, I want you to repeat with me: "Before my bills are due each month, I will take time to reflect on my finances as well as make timely payments to prevent late fees.

<u>Develop a monthly budget:</u>

The number one tip for any parent is to develop a monthly budget. A monthly budget is like having a candle when current (electricity) is turned off. Are you with me? Knowing how much money is coming in and going out each month can be a great eye opener. I believe you never want to spend more than your income. Am I correct or what? In fact, `you should spend less so you can save more. I think I have your attention now, so stay with me and learn how to develop a budget:

Step 1–Since you already know how much income you generate weekly, biweekly, or monthly, write it down as part of the budgeting process. Remember, writing crystallizes thoughts and thoughts motivate actions.

Step 2 – Write down your monthly expenses for rent or mortgage, car payments, gas, light, cable, home phone, cell phone, grocery, public transportation, and any other monthly expenses you may have.

Step 3 - Add all up your expenses for the month and subtract this amount from your income. The remainder/total is the amount you have left for that month to spend and/or save. Attempt to save a minimum of ten percent of your income.

Step 4 - If you want to have more money left at the end of the month, review how much money you spend daily and reduce recurring monthly expenses by eliminating what you can do without. For example, if you are spending too much money on lunch daily you may want to consider carrying lunch from home. Or get rid of your cell phone. If you need one, use a prepaid system instead of signing a contract. Additionally, avoid signing up for ongoing recurring expenses such as joining a gym. These expenses weigh you down like anchors, especially when your income is limited. If you follow this budgeting advice, you will soon have money accruing from monthly savings. Indeed, budgeting is a cost-effective instrument. Do you hear me?

<u>Pay your credit card debt:</u>

The average parent has at least one credit card. Let's not fool ourselves; building credit is an important part of the American culture. Good or bad credit determines if a lender will give you a loan and the interest rate of that loan. However, credit card interest builds up quickly. Therefore, if you have credit card debt, try to remit more than your monthly minimum payment. For a long time now, interest rates on credit cards border around mid-teens. So every $1,000 of credit card debt, for example, could potentially cost you $150 or more per year. Am I making sense?

I believe you have financial goals and dreams like I do. Therefore, in order to keep your head above water, if you know what I mean, paying off high-interest credit card debt is an important step in the right direction. I know debt can accrue for all kinds of reasons. However, the formula for paying credit card debt is pretty simple: Pay more than your monthly minimum and continue settling your debt until your balance is paid off in full. Are you still with me?

<u>Prepare your own food:</u>

To put it plain and simple, fresh, healthy meals are the most budget friendly. Furthermore, there is no meal like a nicely cooked home-made meal. Do you remember the delicious macaroni pie and barbecue chicken your mother or care giver cooked a few weeks, months or years ago? Yes! Think of how delicious they tasted. Think of how she thoroughly cleaned the chicken, chopped up the onions, chive/scallions, and seasoned the chicken overnight. You may have licked your fingers and commented on how delectable the last piece of chicken was. You burped/belched and you felt real good, didn't you?

Your reaction to your mother's cooking was ecstatic because you knew for sure what you were eating, who cooked it and when it was cooked. Are you still with me? The homemade mama's fried chicken is the kind of food preparation I am talking about. Avoid eating out as much as possible. Bag your lunch for work, and stay away from making a stop for coffee every morning. If you start cutting back on the $15 lunches and $2-3 cups of coffee per day, you will be on your way to improving your physical, emotional and financial health. And much like your favorite artist or athlete, your practice of this principle will enable you to become a better manager of your finances. How does that sound to you?

Apart from the physical health and money-saving factors, another benefit of cooking your own food is that it potentially allows you to bond with family members. In that, cooking can become a family activity in which each member plays a role or performs one task. For example, one family member can chop the vegetables, one can stew the chicken, and another can set the table. Are you with me? Cooking, like managing money, requires time and effort. When the family does it together, the burden becomes lighter. Cooking together also allows for family bonding. At the same time, it gives each member an opportunity to contribute to the group effort. Thus, "the family that cooks together stays together." This adage speaks to the potential families have to be more productive, creative and motivated than individuals on their own.

Grocery shop with a list/shop when there is sale:

It is good practice to know what you need to purchase before going to the store. When you go grocery shopping, having a list can make you a much smarter shopper. If you take a shopping list with you and then use it, you will save money. Integral to this process is the commitment to keep track of groceries needed when you run out of an item. In this way, you will have a list of needed items and won't spend money on things that you don't need.

Weekly sale papers are available in most neighborhoods. Take a look at the weekly sale papers to see if there are coupons to match items on your shopping list. You can store your coupons in an envelope in your kitchen cupboard and use them as often as you shop. The use of coupons doesn't mean that you are being cheap. No! on the contrary, you are being frugal. Do you see that? To repeat, shopping with a grocery list enables you to save money. Also, you are more likely not to run out of needed items. This is because you are keeping a running list of dwindling items that will be replaced as needed.

Parents of African descent are encouraged to practice the money management basics in this chapter for three essential reasons:

1. "An alarming number of African-Americans have little or no money saved in retirement accounts and do not own homes, largely because money management has not always been a high priority in a culture that for generations has focused more on civil rights than silver rights" says Sabrina Lamb, author of *Do I look like an ATM? A Parent's Guide to Raising Financially Responsible African-American Children* (Lamb, 2013).
2. Major studies show that African-American families, along with their Hispanic counterparts in the US, still occupy the bottom rung of the economic ladder. This condition points to two things, lack of life skills and knowledge in money management. Practicing the skills suggested in this chapter will enable you to positively impact upward mobility in the Black community (Renford, 2014).
3. Proper money management is the only permanent way to reduce poverty in the Black America says Kelvin Boston – a prominent financial advisor and host of television's syndicated "The Color of Money." In his book, Smart Money Moves for African Americans, he presents down-to-earth advice on investment, entrepreneurship, credit management, and planning for people of color (Boston, 1997).

In his book Outliers: The Story of Success, Malcolm Gladwell gives an amazing account of how extremely successful people achieved success. He accounts for why some people succeed, living remarkably productive and impactful lives, while so many others never reach their potential.

Challenging the cherished belief of the "self-made person," he makes the astounding assertion the superstars don't arise out of nowhere, propelled by genius and talent: "they are not the beneficiaries of hidden advantages and extraordinary opportunities and cultural legacies that allow them to learn and work hard and make sense of the world in ways others cannot." Instead, Gladwell's research proves that it takes roughly ten thousand (10, 000) hours or practice to achieve mastery in any given field (Gladwell, 2011). Using the information in this chapter as a guide, how can parents of African descent leverage Gladwell's idea (practicing money management for 10, 000 hours) to achieve mastery of money management basics?

"Practice makes perfect" is indeed the take away message from this chapter. You can't expect to become a capable money manager overnight, but "practice makes perfect." In other words, doing something over and over again is the only way to learn to do it well. Indeed, training tends to improve performance and change the brain structure, experts say. So, no matter how poised, confident or proficient the world's best cricketers, basketball players, musicians, movie stars, and singers are, these experts became the way they are by adopting this basic tenet: "practice makes perfect." You too, will be a great money manager if you practice being one.

References

Boston, Kelvin. (1997). Smart Money Moves for African-Americans. New York NY: Perigee Trade.

Gladwell, Malcolm. (2011). Outliers: The Story of Success. New York NY: Back Bay Books.

Lamb, Sabrina. (2013). Do I Look Like and ATM? Parents Guide to Raising Financially

Responsible Africa-American Children. Illinois: Lawrence Hill Books.

Renford, Robin. (2014). Income, Savings and opportunities: A Look at Lingering African-American Money Issues. Retrieved November 30, 2014 from http:www.financesonline.com

Appendices

------- O -------

Appendix I

Erickson's Psychosocial Stages of Human Development Summary Chart

Stage	Psychological Crisis & (Virtue)	Important Events	Outcome
Infancy (birth to 18 months)	Trust vs. Mistrust (Hope)	Feeding	Children develop a sense of trust when caregivers provide reliability, care, and affection. A lack of this will lead to mistrust.
Early Childhood (2 to 3 years)	Autonomy vs. Shame and Doubt (Will)	Toilet Training	Children need to develop a sense of personal control over physical skills and a sense of independence. Success leads to feelings of autonomy, failure results in feelings of shame and doubt.
Preschool (3 to 5 years)	Initiative vs. Guilt (Purpose)	Exploration	Children need to begin asserting control and power over the environment. Success in this stage leads to a sense of purpose. Children who try to exert too much power experience disapproval, resulting in a sense of guilt.
School Age (6 to 11 years)	Industry vs. Inferiority (Competency)	School	Children need to cope with new social and academic identity. Success leads to an ability to stay true to yourself, while failure leads to role confusion and a weak sense of self.
Adolescence (12 to 18 years)	Identity vs. Role Confusion (Fidelity)	Social Relationships	Teens need to develop a sense of self and personal identity. Success leads to an ability to stay true to yourself, while failure leads to role confusion and a weak sense of self.
Young Adulthood (19 to 40 years)	Intimacy vs. Isolation (Love)	Relationships	Young adults need to form intimate, loving relationships with other people. Success leads to strong relationships, while failure results in loneliness and isolation.

Middle Adulthood (40 to 65 years)	Generativity vs. Stagnation (Care)	Work and Parenthood	Adults need to create or nurture things that will outlast them, often by having children or creating a positive change that benefits other people. Success leads to feelings of usefulness and accomplishment, while failure results in shallow involvement in the world.
Maturity (65 to death)	Ego Integrity vs. Despair (Wisdom)	Reflection on Life	Older adults need to look back on life and feel a sense of fulfillment. Success at this stage leads to feelings of wisdom, while failure results in regret, bitterness, and despair.

Appendix II

The Food Guidelines

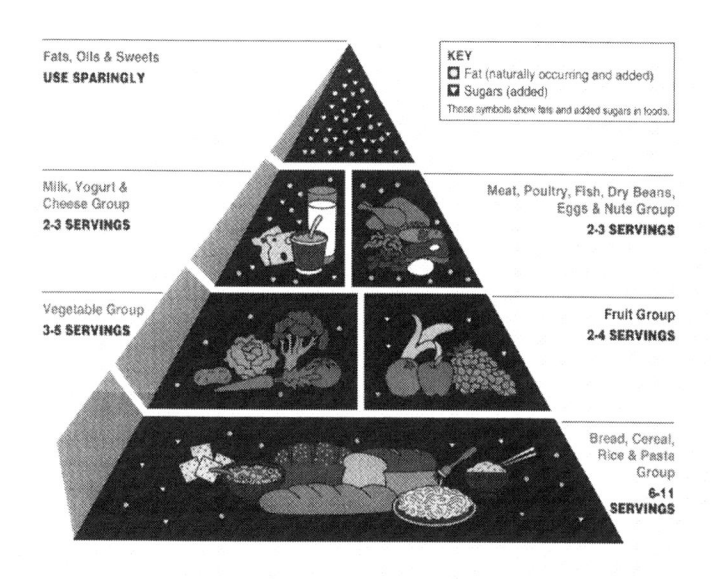

American Heart Association Recommendations for Physical Activity in Adults

Being physically active is important to prevent heart disease and stroke, the nation's No. 1 and No. 5 killers. To improve overall cardiovascular health, we suggest at least 150 minutes per week of moderate exercise or 75 minutes per week of vigorous exercise (or a combination of moderate and vigorous activity). Thirty minutes a day, five times a week is an easy goal to remember. You will also experience benefits even if you divide your time into two or three segments of 10 to 15 minutes per day.

For people who would benefit from lowering their blood pressure or cholesterol, we recommend 40 minutes of aerobic exercise of moderate to vigorous intensity three to four times a week to lower the risk for heart attack and stroke.

Physical activity is *anything* that makes you move your body and burn calories.

This includes things like climbing stairs or playing sports. Aerobic exercises benefit your heart, and include walking, jogging, swimming or biking. Strength and stretching exercises are best for overall stamina and flexibility.

The simplest, positive change you can make to effectively improve your heart health is to start walking. It's enjoyable, free, easy, social and great exercise. A walking program is flexible and boasts high success rates because people can stick with it. It's easy for walking to become a regular and satisfying part of life.

AHA Recommendation

For Overall Cardiovascular Health:

- At least 30 minutes of moderate-intensity aerobic activity at least 5 days per week for a total of 150 minutes

OR

- At least 25 minutes of vigorous aerobic activity at least 3 days per week for a total of 75 minutes; or a combination of moderate- and vigorous-intensity aerobic activity

AND

- Moderate- to high-intensity muscle-strengthening activity at least 2 days per week for additional health benefits.

For Lowering Blood Pressure and Cholesterol

An average 40 minutes of moderate- to vigorous-intensity aerobic activity 3 or 4 times per week

What if I can't make it to the time goal?

Something **is always better than nothing!**

And everyone has to start somewhere. Even if you've been sedentary for years, today is the day you can begin to make healthy changes in your life. If you don't think you'll make it for 30 or 40 minutes, set a reachable goal for today. You can work up toward your overall goal by increasing your time as you get stronger. Don't let all-or-nothing thinking rob you of doing what you can every day.

Appendix IV

Desired Monthly Expenditures (Wants)

Shelter:
    Home renovations or remodeling $_____
    Home furnishings $_____
    Utilities $_____
    Cell phone(s) $_____
    Long-distance phone charges $_____
    Cable or satellite TV $_____
    High-speed Internet $_____

Additional Savings:
    Children's college $_____
    Retirement $_____
    Vehicle replacement fund $_____
    Other financial goals $_____

Food:
    Groceries (beyond basic essentials) $_____
    Dining out $_____
    Meals purchased at school or work $_____
    Snacks and drinks purchased at school or work $_____

Clothing and clothing maintenance: (beyond basic essentials) $_____

Personal:
    Haircuts, color, perms, manicures, massage $_____
    Gifts: Birthday, anniversary, wedding, holiday $_____
    Charitable donations $_____

Entertainment:
    Health club or other club membership(s) $_____
    Vacations $_____
    Summer camp, sports, lessons, hobbies $_____
    Books and magazine and newspaper subscriptions $_____
    Parties: Holiday, birthday, social $_____

Household:
    Home maintenance: Lawn care, exterminators, painters $_____
    Domestic help: House cleaning, babysitters, pet sitters $_____
Transportation: (beyond basic essentials included in Needs)
    Automobile loan or lease payments $_____
    Vehicles and related expenses for children $_____
    Auto maintenance
    Gasoline $_____
    Other: Tolls, parking, public transportation $_____
Total desired additional monthly expenses (Wants) $_____
After-tax income (from Worksheet 3-2, Line 1 – Line 2) $_____
(After-Tax Income - [Total Needs + Total Wants]) $_____
Surplus or Shortfall $_____

Required Monthly Expenses (Needs)

Shelter:
    Home Mortgage or rent $_____
    Utilities $_____
    Electric $_____
    Water, sewer, and trash pickup $_____
    Basic phone service $_____
Protection: Include the things you can't afford to be without.
    Life insurance $_____
    Disability insurance $_____
    Homeowners or renters insurance $_____
    Health insurance $_____
    Auto insurance $_____
    Healthcare/medical and dental care $_____
    Prescription drugs $_____
    Child care $_____
    Rainy-day fund (minimum of 10 percent of gross income) $_____
Food: This category doesn't include dining out
    Groceries (basic essentials only) $_____
Clothing and clothing maintenance: Presuming that you have $_____
some clothes now, ask yourself what else you really need.
Basic Hygiene:
    Personal: Toothbrush, deodorant, soap (for example) $_____
    Household: Laundry detergent, toilet paper, and so on $_____
Transportation:
    Automobile loan or lease payments $_____
    Auto Maintenance $_____
    Gasoline $_____
    Other: Tolls, parking, public transportation $_____
Legal Requirements:
    Real estate and property taxes $_____
    Child support $_____
    Alimony $_____
    Required debt payments not listed elsewhere $_____
    School loans $_____
    Personal loans $_____
    Credit cards $_____
    Other debt $_____
Total required monthly expenses (Needs) $_____
After-tax income (from Worksheet 3-2, Line 1 – Line 2)
Note: If you included all expenses for the household, add the after-tax income of both spouses/partners together
(After-Tax income – Total needs) surplus or shortfall $_____

Cash Flow Monitoring

Item	Month 1	Month 2
Housing		
House Payment	_____	_____
Rent Payment	_____	_____
Lease Payment (not mortgage)	_____	_____
Property improvements	_____	_____
Home association dues	_____	_____
Household incidentals (supplies)	_____	_____
Household Furnishings	_____	_____
Other:	_____	_____
Other:	_____	_____
Subtotal:	_____	_____
Food		
Groceries	_____	_____
Dining out	_____	_____
@ Work	_____	_____
@ School	_____	_____
Other:	_____	_____
Other:	_____	_____
Subtotal:	_____	_____
Clothing		
Clothing	_____	_____
Dry cleaning	_____	_____
Other:	_____	_____
Other:	_____	_____
Subtotal:	_____	_____
Personal Care		
(Hair styling and so on)	_____	_____
Other:	_____	_____
Subtotal:	_____	_____
Automobile		
Monthly payment	_____	_____
Operating expenses (gas, oil, and so on)	_____	_____
Maintenance	_____	_____
Lease Payment	_____	_____
Other:	_____	_____
Subtotal:	_____	_____
Property Tax		
Automobile	_____	_____
House	_____	_____
Boat	_____	_____
Trailer	_____	_____
Other:	_____	_____

Subtotal: _____ _____

Utilities
 Telephone _____ _____
 Cellular phone _____ _____
 Water _____ _____
 Electric _____ _____
 Gas _____ _____
 Trash removal _____ _____
 Cable _____ _____
 Internet _____ _____
 Other: _____ _____
 Other: _____ _____
Subtotal: _____ _____

Entertainment
 Books, newspapers, magazines _____ _____
 Parties (attending or hosting) _____ _____
 Movies (theatre, video, plays, and so on) _____ _____
 Club dues (golf, music, and so on) _____ _____
 Other: _____ _____
 Other: _____ _____
Subtotal: _____ _____

Unreimbursed business expenses
 Travel _____ _____
 Vehicle rentalParking _____ _____
 Lodging _____ _____
 Meals _____ _____
 Entertainment _____ _____
 Other _____ _____
 Other _____ _____
 Subtotal: _____ _____
Alimony (paid)
Subtotal: _____ _____
(Paid)

Child Support
 Subtotal: _____ _____
Children's Expenses
 Lessons, sports, camp, and so on _____ _____
 Daycare _____ _____
 Domestic help (babysitter) _____ _____
 Other: _____ _____
Subtotal: _____ _____

Gifts
 Birthdays _____ _____
 Christmas/ other holiday _____ _____
 Anniversaries _____ _____
 Other: _____ _____
 Other: _____ _____

Subtotal: _____ _____

Charitable Contributions
    (Churches, schools, and so on) _____ _____
    Other: _____ _____
    Other: _____ _____
    Subtotal: _____ _____

Medical Expenses
    Doctor visit copay _____ _____
    Prescription copay _____ _____
    Dental care _____ _____
    Vision Care _____ _____
    Other: _____ _____
    Subtotal: _____ _____

Insurance
    Health _____ _____
    Automobile _____ _____
    Homeowners _____ _____
    Renters _____ _____
    Life _____ _____
    Disability _____ _____
    Long-term care _____ _____
    Umbrella liability _____ _____
    Professional liability _____ _____
    Other: _____ _____
    Other: _____ _____
    Subtotal: _____ _____

Credit Cards
    Credit card #1: _____ _____
    Credit card #2: _____ _____
    Credit card #3: _____ _____
    Credit card #4: _____ _____
    Credit card #5: _____ _____
    Credit card #6: _____ _____
    Other: _____ _____
    Other: _____ _____
    Subtotal: _____ _____

Other Liabilities
    Student loans: _____ _____
    Personal loans: _____ _____
    Business loans: _____ _____
    Other debts: _____ _____
    Other debts: _____ _____
    Subtotal: _____ _____
    TOTAL: _____ _____

Appendix V

Parental Quotations as Affirmations

Quotations or proverbs are succinct motivational statements remembered, spoken of or used by people other than original authors for inspiration, motivation, illustration, illumination and support of their positions, desires or points of view. Used effectively, quotations or proverbs can provide important mind stimulations, give voice to the voiceless, and fresh perspectives to old parenting practices.

In effect, quotations are affirmations we identify with and believe in. In Life 101 McWilliams indicates that "to affirm means to make firm, solid or real. Thoughts, for instance, are not solid. However, when repeated over and over, they become more and more firm. They become feelings, behaviors, methods, experiences and things. "So, when we affirm something, we are either declaring that it is true, giving our support to it or confirming that it is so. For example, what we affirm or believe about parenting has a direct impact on the way we protect, guide and nurture our children.

Using affirmations means to consciously choose quotations that resonate with our spirit or intent to either help eliminate negative habit-patterns or help create positive habit-patterns of living. One way parents can enrich or enhance their parenting style, therefore, is to identify, incorporate and internalize vibrational quotations or proverbs from the collection listed below. The ones adopted will potentially plant affirmational thoughts in your mind. By repeating chosen quotes often enough, you will begin to project their realities outward.

In order to properly understand the phenomena of affirmations, it is necessary to know the science behind how they work. To this end, understand that two distinct states of mind exist within us. Both are intelligent, but while one is conscious the other is unconscious.

The conscious generates ideas and impresses them on the subconscious. The subconscious, in turn, receives these ideas and gives form, meaning and expression to them. All things evolve out of consciousness. By this law, we first conceive and then impress conceived ideas on the subconscious. Without this sequence, there is not anything made that is made.

The conscious impresses the subconscious, while the subconscious expresses all that is impressed upon it. The subconscious does not originate ideas. It accepts as true those which the conscious mind presents to it and then objectifies them.

Affirmations, then, are repetitive quotations that convince the subconscious mind of parents' intentions. Repeated they become beliefs; beliefs become convictions and convictions become action and practice; what's practiced is what's manifested.

Many people mistakenly believe that affirmations are magic wands that bring about effortless changes. Affirmations are not magical. However, they are deliberately stated statements or spiritual tools that keep us constant, boost our potential and enable us to reach our goals by keeping our energies focused on what we say we want to create. Believe it or not, affirmations only work when we put in the work they require. In other words, you can affirm something until the cows come home, but unless you do something significant to round up the cows, they are not coming home.

You are invited, therefore, to engage in activities, practices or rituals that are congruent with your affirmations of choice. Repeat selected quotes or proverbs over and over again until they are internalized. Once you start replacing negative thoughts with positive ones, you will start having positive outcomes.

The following are carefully chosen quotations or proverbs that are appropriate for parents and parenting. You may be able to create your own affirmations; however, they will give you a good start. Be inspired with the treasures of wisdom our ancestors handed down to us. While some of our parents may have forgotten them, the rest of us don't need to

Chapter	Topic	Relevant African Proverbs
01	Love without fear: Building Effective Parent-child Relationships	1. What you help a child to love can be more important than what you help him to learn. ~African Proverb 2. A child brought up where there is always dancing cannot fail to dance. ~Nyanja Proverb 3. Respect a little child, and let him/her respect you. ~Bantu Proverb 4. When a man curses or instills fear in his own child it is a terrible thing. ~African Proverb

02	Roots & Wings: Foundations for Effective Parenting	1. We desire to bequest two things to our children -- the first one is roots; the other one is wings. ~Sudanese Proverb
2. When a child knows how to wash his hands well, he eats with the elders. ~Tshi Proverb
3. If your child is dancing clumsily, tell him: 'you are dancing clumsily'; do not tell him: 'darling, do as you please.' ~Twi Proverb
4. A child who is carried on the back will not know how far the journey is. ~Nigerian Proverb
5. It is the habit that a child forms at home, that follows them to their marriage. ~Nigerian Proverb
6. He who learns, teaches. ~ Ethiopian proverb
7. When a king has good counselors, his reign is peaceful. ~Ashanti proverb
03	Personal Parenting Philosophy	1. A child is what you put into him. ~Nigerian Proverb
2. A child is a child of everyone in the kingdom. ~Sudanese Proverb
3. Patience is the mother of a beautiful child. ~Bantu Proverb
4. When the child falls the mother weeps; when the mother falls the child laughs. ~Rwandan Proverb

04	The Strength Perspective: Playing to Children's Strengths	1. Too large a morsel chokes the child. ~Mauritanian Proverb 2. It's a "bad" child who does not take advice. ~Ashanti Proverb 3. The good mother knows what her children will eat. ~Akan Proverb 4. Parents give birth to the body of their children, but not always to their characters. ~Ganda Proverb
05	Parenting Styles	1. Train a child in the way he should go and make sure you also go the same way. ~African Proverb 2. What the child says, he has heard at home. ~Nigerian Proverb 3. If a mother steals with a child strapped in the back, what do you expect of the child? ~African Proverb
06	The ABC's of Child Development	1. It is not hard to nurse a pregnancy, but it is hard to bring up a child. ~Swahili Proverb 2. When a four-year child is still crawling instead of walking it is time to cry out. ~African Proverb 3. Haste and hurry can only bear children with many regrets along the way. ~Senegalese Proverb 4. By crawling, a child learns to stand. ~West African Proverb

07	Discipline for Dignity: Rewards & Consequences	1. Children will hate all those who give all things to them. ~African Proverb
2. A child who is fearless is going to bring tears to his mother's eyes. ~African Proverb
3. If a child is not well-behaved, she is not sent by the mother to go alone to the market to buy things for her. ~Nigerian Proverb
4. You cannot beat a child to take away its tears. ~African Proverb
5. When you take a knife away from a child, give him a piece of wood instead. ~Kenyan Proverb
6. A child who fears beating, would never admit that he played with a missing knife. ~Nigerian Proverb
7. One should [discipline] a child the first time he comes home with a stolen egg. Otherwise, the day he returns home with a stolen ox, it will be too late. ~Ethiopian Proverb
08	Parent-Child Communication: How to Talk & Listen to Children	1. When you bear a grudge, your child will also bear a grudge. ~Rwandese Proverb
2. You only understand the joys of parenthood when you have your first child, you only understand the mystery of death when in mourning. ~Bahaya Proverb
3. Peace is costly but it is worth the expense. ~Kenyan proverb
4. There can be no peace without understanding. ~Senegalese proverb
5. Having a good discussion is like having riches ~ Kenya

09	Learning Outside The Classroom: Transcending Artificial Boundaries	1. A single hand cannot nurse a child. -Swahili Proverb 2. A child doesn't breastfeed from a stepmother if its mother is still alive. -African Proverb 3. Learning expands great souls. -Namibian proverb 4. If you close your eyes to facts, you will learn through accidents. -African proverb 5. Wealth, if you use it, comes to an end; learning, if you use it, increases. -Swahili proverb 6. Traveling is learning. -Kenyan Proverb 7. Where there are experts there will be no lack of learners. -Swahili Proverb
10	Coping with Parental Stress	1. When a woman has ten children, there is nothing that happens in the night that she does not know about. -Nigerian Proverb 2. It is the duty of children to wait on elders, and not the elders on children. -Kenyan Proverb 3. A child is an axe; when it cuts you, you still pick it up and put it on your shoulder. -Bemba Proverb 4. Only a mother would carry the child that bites her. -Nigerian Proverb 5. Do not make the dress before the child is born. -Tanzanian Proverb

11	Co-Parenting for the Child's Best Outcomes & The Fatherhood Factor: Impact of a Father's Absence	1. A child who has no [father] will not have scars to show on his/her back. ~Nigerian Proverb 2. An immoral [or untrained adoptive father, the traditional step-father, cannot advise his [acquired] children well. ~African Proverb 3. As you do for your ancestors, your children will do for you. ~African Proverb 4. A child does not fear treading on dangerous ground until he or she gets hurt. ~Bukusu Proverb 5. He who fears the crying of a child, will cry himself. ~Swahili Proverb
12	Money Management Basics for Parents	1. The art of negotiating is acquired from childhood. ~Congolese Proverb 2. As you bring up a child, so he will be. ~Swahili Proverb 3. By the time the fool has learned the game, the players have dispersed. ~Ashanti proverb 4. Make some money but don't let money make you. ~ Tanzania 5. It is no shame at all to work for money. ~ Africa 6. He who loves money must labor. ~ Mauritania 7. By labor comes wealth. ~ Yoruba 8. Poverty is slavery. ~Somalia 9. Money is sharper than the sword. – Ashanti 10. Lack of money is lack of friends; if you have money at your disposal, every dog and goat will claim to be related to you. ~ Yoruba 11. You must act as if it is impossible to fail. ~ Ashanti

Appendix VI

Reality-Based Parenting Glossary

A **glossary**, also known as a vocabulary, or lexicon, is an alphabetical list of terms in a particular domain of knowledge with the definitions for those terms. The **glossary** includes terms within the book that are either newly introduced, uncommon, or specialized.

The purpose of this glossary is to provide an accessible dictionary that facilitates a common language relevant to the chapters in Reality-Based Parenting. It is especially for newcomers to this discipline or field of endeavor. Moreover, it contains the working vocabulary and definitions of important or frequently encountered concepts, including idioms or metaphors useful in the study.

Accommodation:	An agreement that allows people, groups, etc., to work together. For example, acceptance of both "minority" and dominant groups of their respective positions in society.
Acculturation:	Acceptance of dominant group values by minority group members
African Diaspora:	Refers to, people of color who descend from the historic forceful and voluntary movements of Africans throughout the world.

Afro–centered:	To maintain African culture as the foundation from which to believe, think, act, speak & behave.
Antagonistic:	Someone or something that opposes and is hostile to a cause.
Archer:	A person who shoot with a bow and arrows.
Assimilation:	To conform or, absorbs as one's own. The gradual loss of distinctiveness of "minority" groups absorbed into dominant population. Maybe of four types – cultural, structural, marital and identificational.
Attainment:	To achieve something through effort.
Attitude:	A fixed way of viewing the world, or a fixed way to think and or feel about something.
Authoritarian:	To favor blind obedience, to favor slave-like obedience.
Authoritative:	To favor child centered approaches.
Awareness:	Identifying, investigating & giving attention to present circumstance.
Capacity:	To possess the uncultivated ability to execute or understand something.
Chattel:	An item of property not real estate.
Cognitive:	That which comes to be known through perception, reasoning, intuition & knowledge.
Commitment:	Having the understanding, discipline & focus to remain dedicated to a worthy person, task or cause.
Competence:	The ability to do something effectively.

Compliance:	To accept an act, process, condition or requirement; the act of conforming, acquiescing, or yielding; the tendency to yield readily to others, especially in a weak and subservient way.
Comprehend:	To grasp with the mind; to understand, able to apply.
Conceptualization:	To develop and clarify a concept, able to use examples to define and illustrate the concept.
Concur:	To agree.
Conformity:	To comply with rules, laws, standards, opinions or etc., usually against one's own will or liking.
Conscientious:	To be fair, thoughtful & thorough.
Conscious:	To have knowledge of yourself, to be awake, aware, to be sensitive of yourself & others, and then to be able to apply what you know.
Contrived:	To deliberately create, through a strained, forced, or unnatural plan.
Crisis:	Opportunity disguised a time of intense danger or difficulty, a turning point and opportunity for change and growth.
Critical:	High level of danger or alert; skillful judgment in seeking truth; judgment towards enhancement.
Crystallize:	To solidify or harden, or to make something clear.
Cultivate:	To improve or develop by education or training; to promote the growth or development of; to give time, thought and effort to; practice; to establish or strengthen.

Culture:	The manifestation of human intelligence, the uniqueness and immune system of a people.
Death instincts:	A primitive impulse for destruction, decay, and death, postulated by Sigmund Freud as coexisting with and opposing the life instinct.
Defiant:	Bold resistance to oppression.
Definiteness:	Clearly defined, very Precise, not vague or general.
Differentiate:	To recognize what makes someone or something different.
Dwindling:	To slowly decrease in size, amount or strength.
Effective:	The best method to produce a desired or intended result.
EGO:	The self; the part of the mind that mediates between the demands of the body and the realities of the environment. The healthy ego finds ways to compromise between these competing pressures and enables the person to cope with the demands of the environment.
Emotional Climate:	Climate is used to describe the emotional system in relationships. There are similarities between the weather and the emotional barometer among people. Emotional climate refers to how emotions are shaped, fostered and changed like the weather does.

Emotional Intelligence:	**Emotional intelligence (EI)** is the ability to monitor one's own and other people's emotions, to discriminate between different emotions and label them appropriately, and to use emotional information to guide thinking and behavior. It is generally said to include 3 skills: 1. Emotional awareness, including the ability to identify your own emotions and those of others; 2. The ability to harness emotions and apply them to tasks like thinking and problems solving; 3. The ability to manage emotions, including the ability to regulate your own emotions, and the ability to cheer up or calm down another person.
Emotionally:	Of or related to the emotion; the subjective, conscious experience characterized primarily by psychophysiological expressions, biological reactions, and mental states.
Empathic:	To understand, to be compassionate.
Exemplifying:	To be a very good example, to show very clearly.
Fictive kin:	A term used to refer to individuals that are unrelated by either birth or marriage, who have an emotionally significant relationship with another individual that would take on the characteristics of a family relationship.
Fidelity:	To be faithful.
Formative:	The developmental process, growing, forming stages.

Frugal: Sparing or economical with regards to money or food.

Functions: The kind of action or activity proper to a person, place or thing.

Genetically: Pertaining or according to genetics; of, relating to, or produced by genes; genic; of, relating to, or influenced by geneses or origins.

Geneticists: A geneticist is a biologist who studies genetics, the science of genes, heredity, and variation of organisms.

Quagmire: An awkward, complex or hazardous situation

Guilt: An emotional reaction to the perception of having done something wrong, having failed to do something, or violating a social norm. The reaction is often a loss of self-esteem and a desire to make restitution.

Habitually: "Habitually" the adjective form of "habit"; a regular tendency or practice.

Humdrum: To lack excitement or variety, dull or boring.

ID: The part of the mind or psyche that harbors the individual's instinctive or biological drives, libido, or psychic energy.

Identity: An individual's sense of self and of uniqueness as well as the basic integration and continuity of values, behavior, and thoughts that are maintained in varied circumstances.

Identity Confusion: Lack of direction and definition of self.

Impelled: The drive, force or urge to do something.

Inception:	The establishment or starting point, the beginning, birth or origin.
Indefinite:	Not clearly expressed or defined, or lasting for an unknown on unstated length of time.
Induce:	To succeed in persuading, or to bring about or give rise to.
Industrious:	To be hard-working, to work tirelessly
Inferior:	Something lower in quality
Initiative:	The ability to assess and initiate things independently
Inter-personal:	Between people.
Intimacy:	A close familiarity or friendship.
Intra Personal:	Occurring within the individuals mind or self
Intrinsic:	Essential or natural; belonging to the essential nature or constitution of a person or thing.
Isolation:	The state of being in a place or situation that is separate from other
Kinesthetic:	Learning through feeling, touching and movement.
Life and Death instinct:	Sigmund Freud determined that all instincts fall in one of two major classes: **the life instincts** and **the death instincts**. The life or sexual instincts are those that deal with basic survival, pleasure, and reproduction. These instincts are important for sustaining the life of the individual as well as the continuation of the species. While they are often called sexual instincts, these drives also include such things like thirst, hunger, and pain avoidance. The energy created by life instincts is known as libido. Freud also

proposed that "the goal of life is death. He noted that after people experience a traumatic event (such as war), they often reenact the experience. He concluded that people hold an unconscious desire to die but that this wish is largely tempered by the life instincts.

Maafa: The African Holocaust; the deliberate actions or systems set up to keep Africans people degenerated, wounded and left in poverty.

Mechanism: A system of parts working together; a system for achieving a result; a mechanical operation or action.

Metaphor: A figure of speech in which a word or a phrase is applied to something to which it is not literally applicable in order to show a likeness e.g. England is the mother country; a mighty fortress is our God (fortress = a secured place, a stronghold, a fortified place with exceptional security.

Methodology: A body of methods and rules applied to a project or idea.

Modalities: The way something exist, or the way a thing is experienced or expressed.

Myriad: A very large number of things.

Neophyte: An apprentice, or novice.

Objective: To base on facts rather than feelings or opinions, not influenced by feelings.

Optimize: To make or do something as effective as possible.

Parents: A parent is a caretaker of the offspring in their own species. In humans, a parent is of a child (where "child" refers to offspring, not necessarily age).

Pathologically:	To be extreme in a way that is not normal or that shows an illness or mental problem.
Perception:	The way an individual sees the world, or views a thing.
Permissive:	To allow excessive freedom of behaviors.
Perpetuate:	To make perpetual or cause to last indefinitely; for example, continue or preserve a not fully measured belief.
Philosophies:	A particular system of thoughts and beliefs.
Political Dynamics:	The chemistry or intangible working among parties.
Postulate:	A statement accepted as true for the purposes of a discussion, argument or debate.
Potential:	Having the capacity to develop or become into something.
Procreation:	To give birth to, to bring forth, to reproduce.
Psychologically:	Relating to the inner working of the mind.
Readymade:	For a thing to be available on demand, prepared in advance.
Reality-based Parenting:	The art of perceiving things as they are and not as they might appear to be.
Reciprocal:	Describing a relationship or interaction where both sides agree to do similar things for each other, to allow each other the same rights, to be fair on both sides.
Reciprocity:	To reward each other at approximately equal rates.
Reconciliation:	The process of finding a way to become friendly again or to no longer be in conflict.

Regression:	A stage of growth, where one temporarily returns to previous undesired behaviors, thoughts etc.
Relationship:	A commitment two or more people make with each other to achieve a thing or desired goal.
Relevant:	Relating to a subject in an appropriate way.
Responsibility:	To be accountable for something, or to have an accountable, dependable or trust worthy character.
Rigid:	A hard, unbending, or uncompromising person, place or thing. Not flexible.
Rudimentary:	To be basic or simple
Self:	The self is the subject of one's own experience of phenomena: perception, emotions, and thoughts. In phenomenology, it is conceived as *what* experiences, and there isn't any experiencing without an experience, the self.
Self-Esteem:	The opinion or definition of one's self. In other words, it reflects a person's overall emotional evaluation of his or her own worth. It is a judgment of oneself as well as an attitude toward the self. Self-esteem encompasses beliefs (for example, "I am competent," "I am worthy") and emotions such as triumph, despair, pride and shame. 'The self-concept is what we think about the self; self-esteem, is the positive or negative evaluations of the self.
Sensitive:	To be delicate or easily disturbed.

Sentiment:	A view of or attitude towards a situation, event or opinion.
Synthesized:	To combine so as to form a new, complex product; to form or produce by chemical synthesis or to produce (sound or music) by means of a synthesizer.
Social Structures:	Manmade or man determined systems, beliefs, and behaviors.
Socialization:	How one is conditioned to react or respond to certain situations, behaviors or beliefs.
Socio-economic:	Situations influenced by or related to a combination of social and economic factors.
Superego:	The part of the psyche or personality that regulates the individual's ethical standards, conscience, and sense of right and wrong. The superego is said to begin its development by identifying with the apparent values and rules established by parent- figures.
Sustainable:	To be able to last or continue for a long time without completely diminishing.
Syndrome:	A group of sign and symptoms that occur together, that characterize a particular abnormality or condition.
Tactile:	Able to touch.
Tantamount:	To be equivalent to something.
Temperaments:	The usual attitude, mood, or behavior of a person or animal.
Trauma:	Trauma is the experience of stress which is prolonged, overwhelming and unpredictable.

Trauma triangle:	The trauma triangle is the psychological concept of unexpressed or repressed attitudes, feelings and behaviors about how people, all people, can get hooked into the angles of the triangle. Trauma, in this case, is ultimately manifested as one or more of the following: anger, depression or passive/aggressive behaviors.
Trust:	Firm belief in the integrity, ability, or character of a person or thing; confidence or reliance
Utero:	The Uterus
Valued:	To have high regard for people, places and things; to be protected and maintained out of respect, necessity and desire.
Vocation:	The work one spends their entire life doing.
Zealous:	To have passion in one movement.

Appendix VII

Notable Books

20 Inspirational Works

The list that follows contains books, which have been requested by parents who have completed Reality-Based Parenting classes. Many works in the collection have been great guides and mentors in their personal and parental growth. It is an honor to share these priceless gems that have inspired, motivated, and initiated internal revolutions for many parents. These gems are relevant resources that provide practical help and valuable lessons parents can use to enhance their skills. Other benefits that can be derived from reading selected books are vocabulary expansion and imagination stimulation.

Every individual has his or her own taste. Many parents have found something beautiful, inspiring, and motivating in these books. To those who are seeking optimal parenting help this book list can be a treasure.

Please create some time to read some or all of the books listed below. The order does not matter. You can start with any one and soon you will experience enhancement in your consciousness and parenting style. These books will challenge you, frustrate you, and inspire you. In the end, you will be grateful that they exist and are available to you.

<u>Achebe, Chinua</u>: <u>Things Fall Apart</u>. *This book* tells two intertwining stories, both centering on Okonkwo, a "strong man" of an Ibo village in

Nigeria. The first, a powerful fable of the immemorial conflict between the individual and society, traces Okonkwo's fall from grace with the tribal world. The second, as modern as the first, concerns the clash of cultures and the destruction of Okonkwo's world with the arrival of aggressive European missionaries. These perfectly harmonized twin dramas are informed by an awareness capable of encompassing at once the life of nature, human history, and the mysterious compulsions of the soul.

<u>Akbar, Na'im Dr.</u>: <u>From Mis-education to Education</u>. This book is considered a must read for anyone involved in the education of Blacks living in White dominated countries. The author does well to point out the shortcomings of a Euro-centric teaching structure that leaves out consideration for black culture and heritage. This has resulted in blacks being truly mis-educated and has caused many to live in complete contradiction to their own best interests. This book strongly points out the importance of Black history and culture, and its absence in mainstream educational systems.

<u>Butch Slaughter & Grimes, Eric K</u>: <u>Why Our Children Hate Us</u>. Why our children hate us explores the systemic means and methods Black adults unwittingly and sometimes intentionally employ to the detriment of their own children. Through a collection of vignettes, interviews and reflections, the book examines the impact of the Civil Rights-era, embedded racism, media and religion on the future chances of Black children. Why our children hate us includes various brief, yet intense passages focused on incarceration of Black youth, religious neglect of Black youth and the educational marginalization of Black youth. The selection of succinct, sardonic reflections is masterfully rounded out by two engaging interviews including one with Civil Rights veteran activist Colia Clark.

<u>Comeer James P. &Puissant, Alvin F.</u>: <u>Raising black children</u>. The authors explore central psychological, social, and educational aspects of child development from infancy through adolescence. They address problems and situations peculiar to raising an African American child in a predominantly White society. Topics discussed include how to cope with racism, the pros and cons of busing, and universal child - rearing concerns. Many issues overlooked in traditional parenting manuals,

such as the absent parent, gang involvement, and teenage sexuality, are treated here with admirable candor and directness. The importance of developing a child's self-esteem, sense of security, and racial and personal pride is affirmed throughout.

Edwards, Haskell G.: The immigrant Family. Dr. Edwards provides an exceptional framework for adaptation and excellence. He argues that immigrant parents would do well to reflect on their historical and sociological backgrounds in order to better understand the influences from the past that impact the challenges of parenting in a new culture.

Garvey, Marcus: Message to the people: The Course of African Philosophy. In September 1937, three years before his death, Marcus Garvey assembled a small group of his most trusted organizers. For almost a quarter of a century, he had led the Universal Negro Improvement Association, the largest international mass movement in the history of African peoples. Now he wanted to pass on the lessons he had learned, to the group best suited to carry the struggle forward. For one month, he instructed this elite student body, twelve hours a day, seven days a week. The sessions were secret and much of the instruction was not written down. The students did, however receive written copies of twenty-two lessons, which Garvey called the Course of African Philosophy. This fascinating distillation of a great leader's experience is here written.

Glen, Steven H., & Nelson, Jane: Raising Self-Reliant Children in a Self-Indulgent World: Seven Building Blocks for Developing Capable Young People. Bestselling authors have helped hundreds of thousands of parents raise capable, independent children with Raising Self-Reliant Children in a Self-Indulgent World. On its tenth anniversary, this parenting classic returns with fresh, up-to-date information to offer parents inspiring and workable ideas for developing a trusting relationship with children, as well as the skills to implement the necessary discipline to help children become responsible adults. Those who think in terms of leniency versus strictness will be surprised. This book goes beyond these issues to teach children to be responsible and self-reliant—not through outer-directed concerns, such as fear and intimidation, but through inner-directed behavior, such as feeling accountable for one's commitments. The book shows parents how to instill character-building values and traits in children that last a lifetime. During these turbulent days when families are in disarray and children are getting the short end of the stick, this book can be very helpful to parents who are desirous of bring up self-reliant children with a formula for developing closeness, trust, dignity, and respect.

Goggins, Lathardus: African centered rites of passage and education. Discussing the correlation between one's self-conception and one's academic performance, this book explains African centered rites and the rituals and ceremonies behind them.

Hill, Paul: Coming of age. This book explores an important aspect of coming of age, and examines how the Black community can institutionalize rites of passage as part of the child-rearing processes and practices.

James, George G.M.: Stolen Legacy. George Granville Monah James, a South American historian and author, best known for his book Stolen Legacy, in which he argued that Greek philosophy originated in ancient Egypt. "The term 'Greek philosophy,' to begin with is a misnomer, for there is no such philosophy in existence. The ancient Egyptians had developed a very complex religious system, called the Mysteries, which was also the first system of salvation. "As such, it regarded the human body as a prison house of the soul, which could be liberated from its bodily impediments, through the disciplines of the Arts and Sciences, and advanced from the level of a mortal to that of a God. This was the notion of the summumbonum or greatest good, to which all men must aspire, and it also became the basis of all ethical concepts. The Egyptian Mystery System was also a Secret Order, and membership was gained by initiation and a pledge to secrecy. The teaching was graded and delivered orally to the Neophyte; and under these circumstances of secrecy, the Egyptians developed secret systems of writing and teaching, and forbade their Initiates from writing what they had learnt. "After nearly five thousand years of prohibition against the Greeks, they were permitted to enter Egypt for the purpose of their education."

Johnson, Charles: Middle Passage. Rutherford Calhoun, a newly freed slave and irrepressible rogue, is lost in the underworld of 1830s New Orleans. Desperate to escape the city's unscrupulous bill collectors and the pawing hands of a schoolteacher hell-bent on marrying him, he jumps aboard the *Republic*, a slave ship reroute to collect members of a legendary African tribe, the Allmuseri. Thus begins a voyage of metaphysical horror and human atrocity, a journey which challenges our notions of freedom, fate, and how we live together. Peopled with vivid and unforgettable characters, nimble in its interplay of comedy and serious ideas, this dazzling modern classic is a perfect blend of the picaresque tale, historical romance, sea yarn, slave narrative, and philosophical allegory.

Kafele, Baruti K.: A Black parent handbook to Educating your children. A Black Parent's Handbook to Educating Your Children is a guide describing ways in which parents can play a much more active and productive role towards children's educational growth and development at home. Throughout the Black community, there is a tremendous amount of debate and discussion about the problems of the public school system, and its impact on the future of "our" children. This necessitates the need for parents to maintain maximum involvement.

Kunjufu, Jawanza Dr.: Developing positive self-images & Discipline in Black children. An excellent read and a must have for all African-American families. The book guides parents and others in our community on ways to navigate through a system that is not geared for the positive growth and development of Black children. It gives us positive ways to overcome this system without condemning the system itself.

Lewis, Mary C.: Herstory Black Female Rites of Passage. Providing a wealth of information about the physical, social, emotional, and cultural development of young Black females, this volume attempts to answer the question, *When does a girl become a woman?*

Murphy, Joseph Dr.: The Power of Your Subconscious Mind. DR. Joseph Murphy wrote, taught, counseled, and lectured to thousands of people all over the world for nearly fifty years. In the preface, Dr. Joseph Murphy asserts that life events are actually the result of the workings of your conscious and subconscious minds. He suggests practical techniques through which one can change one's destiny, principally by focusing and redirecting this miraculous energy.

Years of research studying the world's major religions convinced him that some great Power lay behind all spiritual life and that this power is within each of us. Dr. Murphy remains a beacon of enlightenment and inspiration for legions of loyal followers. The Power of Your Subconscious Mind has been a bestseller since its first publication in 1963, selling many millions of copies since its original publication.

Shapiro, Lawrence E.: How to Raise a Child with a High EQ: A Parents' Guide to Emotional Intelligence. Studies show that emotional intelligence -- the social and emotional skills that make up what we call character -- is more important to your child's success than the cognitive intelligence measured by IQ. And unlike IQ, emotional intelligence can be developed in kids at all stages.

Filled with games, checklists, and practical parenting techniques, *How to Raise a Child with a High EQ* will help you to help your child cope with -- and overcome -- the emotional stress of modern times and the normal problems of growing up.

Ouspensky, P.D.: The Psychology of Man's Possible Evolution. The book studies humans in view of what he/she may become. It describes how a man or woman must work simultaneously on their knowledge and their being to find inner unity. In his book, the psyche is "the soul or spirit" and psychology the means of human evolution to a higher level of awareness and being. This is not what is being taught in schools, as Ouspensky points out. He postulates that there is a "true self" one must get to know. However, we will not advance until we acknowledge that we are "machines." We must undo our machine-like ways before we can become free. This freeing from the hard-wiring of our natures is possible through inherent abilities to not only comprehend and envision, but to turn these into action.

Williams Norissa J PhD: Get Your Life!: A Quick & Easy Guide to Help You Set Your Goals and Write Personal Mission & Vision Statements to Live Your Dreams (Tools for Living)

Get Your Life! is like hiring a life coach for a fraction of the cost! Whether you are looking to start a business or lose weight, Get Your Life! It is a quick and easy guide with simple processes to help you get to the core of who you are, what makes you happy and what you want to do in life. It's perfect for any age and can help you chart your course with both large and small goals. Make this year your best year by living your best life.

<u>Wilson N Amos</u>: <u>Awakening the Natural Genius of Black Children</u>. Dr. Wilson's premise is that there are natural talents residing in Black children from birth. By connecting this innate genius to the profound purpose of Black survival and empowerment, we can bring these children to a point where they will desire to awaken and develop their own genius potential.

<u>Woodson, Carter G.</u>: <u>The Mis-Education of the Negro</u>. The thesis of Dr. Woodson's book is that African-Americans of his day were being culturally indoctrinated, rather than taught, in American schools. This conditioning, he claims, causes African-Americans to become dependent and to seek out inferior places in the greater society of which they are a part. He challenges his readers to become autodidacts and to "do for themselves", regardless of what they were taught: History shows that it does not matter who is in power... those who have not learned to do for themselves and have to depend solely on others never obtain any more rights or privileges in the end than they did in the beginning.

Index

A

Abandoned 129
acceptance 22, 49, 53, 62, 128, 175
adaptive 33, 112, 114, 118, 119
African ix, xi, xii, xiii, xv, xvii, 1, 2, 3, 5, 6, 7, 9, 10, 11, 12, 20, 21, 23, 24, 30, 33, 36, 39, 48, 53, 54, 56, 57, 59, 62, 64, 65, 66, 67, 68, 70, 71, 74, 75, 76, 89, 92, 94, 95, 96, 112, 113, 114, 115, 123, 124, 126, 129, 131, 142, 143, 145, 150, 151, 152, 170, 171, 172, 173, 174, 175, 176, 182, 188, 189, 190, 191, 193
agreements 69
apprenticeship 25
assessment 68, 87, 89, 97, 98
attachment 7, 8, 9, 118
Attachment 8, 9, 10, 72
average 12, 148, 160

B

Black 2, 3, 5, 8, 9, 10, 24, 28, 54, 62, 64, 76, 86, 89, 97, 99, 113, 120, 129, 131, 150, 188, 190, 191, 193
blended families 117, 118, 122
bonding 8, 73, 149
budget 143, 146, 147, 148

C

chattel slavery 7, 54, 70, 78
children vii, xi, xii, xiii, xiv, 1, 2, 3, 5, 6, 7, 8, 9, 10, 11, 12, 13, 14, 15, 16, 17, 19, 20, 21, 22, 23, 24, 25, 26, 27, 28, 29, 30, 31, 32, 33, 34, 35, 38, 39, 47, 48, 49, 50, 51, 54, 55, 56, 57, 58, 59, 60, 61, 62, 65, 66, 68, 70, 71, 73, 74, 75, 76, 77, 78, 79, 80, 81, 82, 85, 86, 87, 88, 89, 91, 92, 93, 97, 101, 112, 113, 114, 116, 118, 119, 120, 121, 122, 123, 124, 125, 126, 127, 128, 129, 130, 131, 143, 162, 167, 170, 171, 173, 174, 188, 189, 191, 193
commitment xii, 24, 62, 75, 149, 184
Communication xvi, 26, 74, 78, 79, 80, 84, 112
conflict 26, 58, 95, 96, 98, 117, 118, 119, 121, 126, 183, 188
conscious parents 48
Consequences xvi, 65, 172
CO-PARENTING 116

195

core values 11
corporal punishment 54, 66, 76, 77, 78
crisis 59, 67, 73, 123
cultural ix, xi, xii, xiii, 2, 5, 12, 20, 22, 23, 28, 29, 34, 58, 62, 68, 75, 89, 101, 113, 114, 131, 142, 151, 176, 191
cultural accommodation 62
cultural competency xi, 68
culturally grounded xiii, 16
cultural values 20, 58
culture xix, 5, 14, 15, 21, 29, 32, 36, 47, 48, 58, 75, 76, 78, 91, 92, 97, 98, 131, 143, 148, 150, 176, 188, 189

D

death instinct 3
death-life instinct 2
developmental needs 28, 100
developmental stages 21, 27, 57, 62, 101
dialogue 12, 28, 78, 79, 80, 81, 99, 118, 121
Discipline xvi, 28, 64, 65, 67, 68, 70, 71, 84, 172, 191
distress 8
domains 34, 35

E

education xi, xiv, 13, 15, 17, 20, 21, 23, 24, 39, 58, 76, 85, 89, 90, 91, 93, 122, 145, 177, 188, 190
Effectively 20
emotional climate 12, 26, 47, 48, 53, 82, 101
emotional intelligence 192
empowered 34, 69
end in mind 68, 146
enthusiasm vii, 8, 22

F

family ix, xii, 5, 8, 9, 11, 13, 17, 22, 23, 25, 27, 55, 62, 66, 67, 68, 69, 70, 73, 79, 82, 86, 89, 95, 97, 98, 100, 101, 117, 118, 120, 122, 124, 125, 129, 130, 131, 143, 146, 149, 179
feedback vii, xi, 74
financial game plan 143
Forgiveness 23

G

goals ix, 16, 22, 31, 32, 33, 34, 36, 47, 58, 61, 62, 67, 68, 69, 98, 131, 146, 148, 161, 168, 193
guilt 2, 60, 69

H

Human technology skills 26

I

independence 11, 12, 15, 26, 32, 52, 60, 62
Insight 12
intelligence 39, 40, 54, 81, 178, 179, 192
intentional 34, 35
internalized 11, 126, 168
intrinsic motivation 71, 91

L

leadership ix
learning 6, 24, 25, 26, 27, 58, 61, 67, 71, 85, 86, 87, 89, 90, 91, 92, 93, 94, 95, 127, 132, 173
love xiv, 1, 2, 3, 5, 6, 7, 8, 9, 17, 22, 49, 62, 71, 83, 92, 94, 99, 128, 170

M

manhood 127
metaphor 25, 29
modeling 14, 81, 124
money management skills 146
motivation 87, 90, 167

N

Nature 37, 38, 58
Nurture 37, 38, 58

P

Parenting vii, ix, x, xi, xii, xiii, xv, xvi, xvii, 11, 15, 19, 20, 28, 29, 30, 31, 36, 38, 47, 48, 49, 50, 51, 52, 54, 55, 56, 57, 70, 88, 94, 101, 115, 122, 131, 170, 171, 174, 175, 183, 187
parenting investment strategies 32
parenting philosophy 16, 31, 35, 53
parenting practices 33, 47, 48, 53, 54, 118, 167
parenting styles 47, 48, 53, 54, 66, 131
passionate learning 92
paying attention 88
positive alliance 119
potential 12, 13, 16, 37, 38, 57, 61, 63, 73, 101, 149, 150, 168, 193
practice xii, xiii, 6, 13, 22, 49, 66, 76, 80, 90, 145, 146, 149, 150, 151, 168, 177, 180
problems 9, 15, 24, 25, 50, 52, 66, 69, 73, 76, 95, 102, 118, 123, 128, 131, 179, 188, 191, 192
psycho-spiritual 129
punishment 6, 7, 8, 9, 23, 24, 49, 51, 53, 54, 66, 70, 71, 76, 77, 78, 84, 97

Q

questions 19, 35, 38, 74, 81, 86, 89, 92, 95, 124

R

racial socialization 33, 113, 115
Reality-Based Parenting xii
relationship 2, 5, 8, 48, 51, 53, 57, 62, 67, 74, 76, 79, 81, 82, 117, 118, 119, 128, 129, 130, 131, 179, 183, 189
Relationships xi, xv, 2, 3, 6, 10, 170
resolution 98, 120, 121
responsibility 2, 11, 12, 13, 16, 19, 28, 49, 69, 70, 75, 97, 117, 119, 142, 143, 146
role confusion 28, 61, 62, 100, 117
roles 28, 31, 52, 62, 70, 95, 96, 97, 114, 118, 119, 121, 123, 125, 126, 131
Roots xv, 11, 12, 19, 20, 27, 29, 87, 170

S

savings 148
Self-Care 112
self-control 5, 24, 51, 55, 66
self-denial 145
self-esteem 6, 50, 52, 54, 61, 114, 124, 126, 180, 184, 189
sensitivity 40, 82
shortfall 163
societal 21, 39, 123
strengths xii, 5, 14, 22, 38, 40, 59, 75, 88, 91
stress 70, 73, 94, 95, 97, 98, 101, 102, 114, 115, 185, 192
stress buffers 102
Stress management 102

support vii, ix, 12, 13, 20, 22, 34, 60, 69, 70, 87, 97, 99, 101, 117, 128, 163, 167

T

training xiv, 2, 19, 20, 25, 26, 68, 146, 151, 177
triangulation 117, 118, 119, 120

U

unconditional love 25, 83
upward mobility 150

V

vacation 89, 102
value xii, xiv, 8, 13, 14, 16, 17, 23, 25, 53, 68, 78, 79, 82, 89, 91, 98, 114, 127
value-based 79
values 8, 11, 12, 13, 15, 16, 17, 21, 22, 25, 31, 33, 34, 39, 51, 53, 75, 78, 82, 90, 92, 97, 113, 114, 175, 180, 185, 190
value system xii, 13, 14, 53

W

Wings xv, 11, 15, 20, 25, 27, 87, 170

Printed in Great Britain
by Amazon